Cambridge Elements

Elements in Business Strategy
edited by
J.-C. Spender
Rutgers Business School

HIGH VELOCITY BUSINESS OPERATIONS

Yemmanur Jayachandra
Wireless Wearables

CAMBRIDGE
UNIVERSITY PRESS

CAMBRIDGE
UNIVERSITY PRESS

University Printing House, Cambridge CB2 8BS, United Kingdom

One Liberty Plaza, 20th Floor, New York, NY 10006, USA

477 Williamstown Road, Port Melbourne, VIC 3207, Australia

314–321, 3rd Floor, Plot 3, Splendor Forum, Jasola District Centre,
New Delhi – 110025, India

79 Anson Road, #06–04/06, Singapore 079906

Cambridge University Press is part of the University of Cambridge.

It furthers the University's mission by disseminating knowledge in the pursuit of
education, learning, and research at the highest international levels of excellence.

www.cambridge.org
Information on this title: www.cambridge.org/9781108811675
DOI: 10.1017/9781108867801

© Yemmanur Jayachandra 2020

First published 2020

A catalogue record for this publication is available from the British Library.

ISBN 978-1-108-81167-5 Paperback
ISSN 2515-0693 (online)
ISSN 2515-0685 (print)

High Velocity Business Operations

Elements in Business Strategy

DOI: 10.1017/9781108867801
First published online: August 2020

Yemmanur Jayachandra
Wireless Wearables
Author for correspondence: Yemmanur Jayachandra, pjayachand@gmail.com

Abstract: This Element deals with the know-how and show-how to accomplish high velocity business operations. The basis of these operations is real-time data and low latency processing. Relevant applications are pervasive due to the emerging technologies of IoT, 5G, AI and data analytics. This Element explores theories and methods of configuring, formulating and implementing high velocity business operations with properly designed and developed platforms and processes.

Current mobile transformation is enabling the unwiring of businesses, de-territorializing them, and creating more opportunities for these operations. High velocity business processes increase throughput and efficiency, offering first-mover advantage. They also provide location independence due to use of mobile platforms and devices (smartphones, tablets and wearables). This Element presents mobility as a critical attribute of high velocity business operations, taking advantage of worldwide resources and expertise with well-designed mobile platforms and their data.

Key Words: mobile business, real-time business, faster-than-real-time, platforms, mobile platforms, mobile moments, high velocity business, high speed streaming data analytics, unwiring the business.

ISBNs: 9781108811675 (PB), 9781108867801 (OC)
ISSNs: 2515-0693 (online), 2515-0685 (print)

Contents

1 Introduction

This Element deals with high velocity business strategies to accomplish high efficiency, accelerated, real-time, and faster-than-real-time business processes in order to achieve higher productivity to out-perform competition. It is important to note that high velocity business operations necessary for these strategies can only take place when a company's inputs from its suppliers and its outputs of products and services are fully digitized and exposed to wireless networks and access devices like handheld mobile smartphones and iPads. Real-time data acquisition and processing with high-speed communications with fast processors is essential.

High velocity business operations are accomplished by the combination of three fundamental technologies: 1. high-speed computing; 2. high-velocity and high-bandwidth networks such as fiber landline and 5G wireless with high connectivity between concerned objects (as by IoT); and 3. innovative formulation of business tasks. While items 1 and 2 are confined to computing and networking companies, item 3 is generic to several businesses. Therefore, we have emphasized item 3 more here.

High velocity business processes play a pivotal role for competitive advantage as a first mover and to radically transform a business for new opportunities (Spear, 2009; Steinberg, 2016). High velocity only assures initial instantaneous competitive advantage, but its second-and higher-order derivatives, such as higher accelerations, are more relevant for accomplishing dominant position in the business field. A deer's initial high speed can be easily surpassed by a tiger with lower initial velocity but higher later acceleration. Therefore, higher-order derivatives of velocity, like acceleration, are more important than original high velocity.

It is important to note that a single business operation or transaction will trigger many multiples of suboperations, transactions and tasks that also must be performed at high velocities with relevant coordination and context. A simple operation of addressing a customer order will trigger customer payment processes, inventory lookup, shipping and the like, which involve many internal and external organizational suboperations. Similarly, a business industrial operation can trigger several suboperations of manufacturing and assembling processes and events that require coordination with multiple parties of supplier chains and internal departments.

The current way of conducting many business operations is based on PCs as workhorses and back-end servers of large computer groups. They are expensive, tedious and location dependent. A high velocity business enterprise migrates such operations to simple mobile smartphone devices and cloud computing, as we will discuss further in this Element. The emerging standards and technologies of Internet of Things (IoT), 5G, AI (Kapoor, 2019; Pathak and Bhandari, 2018) and data analytics are stimulating numerous applications, like autonomous vehicles, remote factory control with robots, sensors and actuators, and increasing the velocity of business operations by several orders of magnitude.

High velocity operations depend on wireless mobility and mobile moment's interactions with stakeholders. This is an exciting field and this Element deals with how to transform any business through high-speed mobility with wireless devices and platforms to a new level currently not achieved. It provides new vision and insights based on the fundamental concepts of mobility and platforms in order to achieve improvements in cost reductions, higher speeds of conducting business through real-time business processes and many faster-than-real-time business processes. It deals with all aspects of enterprise mobility and associated mobile platforms as applicable to modern enterprises and businesses wishing to exploit the new digital world.

1.1 Importance of Mobile Devices

Today's greatest challenge is to attain more value, efficiency and speed in conducting a business with inexpensive and commoditized devices like smartphones rather than the current PC-based business processes. Electronic mobility is the essential enabler to accomplish it. This Element addresses this challenge and provides several examples.

Business success and prosperity depends on the ability to formulate and incorporate many high velocity business operations throughout the physical and networked working space of the enterprise. Our material relationships to the current world are through our senses and knowledge acquired by probing our surroundings with vital networks of knowledge generated, transacted and exchanged instantaneously, anywhere and at any time. Smartphone wireless networks are effective ways to utilize a variety of sensors and their associated activators. They enable us to provide actionable cyber spaces with sensor swarms and sensor-actuator networks, where we can work and allow us to manipulate objects at remote places on the globe with high speed and velocity.

Far more important is our ability to collect and use pertinent data from a variety of sources that must be universally distributed and instantly accessible for everyday business operations by our human senses as well as with super-human smartphone sensors. Therefore, smartphones play a vital role in many businesses, augmenting our real world with measured observations, information and knowledge.

We are now at the turning point in our human development where we are migrating from the mere cyberspace of knowledge to an action-based, sensor-networked world with the aid of smartphones. Our individual and business success depends on our ability to navigate the digital world's knowledge space and, more importantly, using appropriate sensors and manipulating the physical world with the help of the knowledge space, to desired outcomes. We have just conquered the knowledge space of the physical world with the aid of the Internet and Web-browsing processes. The unfinished task before us is now to autonomously sense and manipulate the physical world through the knowledge space we have already acquired. Smartphones with their sensors and processing elements are the powerful tools to accomplish this mission through their precise measurements and observations.

1.2 New Nomads: Global Itinerant Immigrants

We have now become new nomads to seek and perform work at any place on earth. The more we can easily and remote-autonomously manipulate the physical world through intelligent spaces of embedded and external smartphone sensors with their rapid response, the more we will be assured success in today's hypercompetitive environment. It is also important that our material relationships to the physical world are maintained through a well-connected and logical infrastructure of institutions and organizations like business corporations, governmental, semi-governmental, welfare, educational and training institutions, and social networks for which smartphones provide ample applications and services. These well-connected resources play a vital role in performing high velocity business operations.

The interconnection of smartphones and sensors with computers and storage systems over the Internet will continue to expand the digitized cyberworld with the sensor-digitized physical world for action-oriented remote and autonomous manipulation of our surroundings and the globe at large. Virtualization and contextualization play a vital role in such a sensor-actualized physical world. The fusion of sensed information, communications, informatics, the Internet and cloud computing are the inevitable consequences of the commercialization and monetization of advanced high velocity operations of smartphone apps. New patterns of remote and autonomous manipulation of our physical world through the cyberspace world have important consequences on our civilization and they must be regulated and performed in cooperation with many persons and organizations with vested interests. Governments, corporations and individuals are soon facing socio-economic and cultural choices in this endeavor. The future is predicated on our willingness to shape the sensor-actuated digital world with the knowledge-based world and develop them both for mutual advantages to all of us.

1.3 Disembodied Devices: Disrupting Established Industries

A smartphone can create multiple virtual devices (Somayaji et al., 2014) through mobile virtualization schemes within itself, like personal computers, television, tablets, multiple smartphone device configurations and the like. These virtual devices can act as actual physical devices, although they are disembodied and exist in a virtual space of a smartphone screen. The smartphone is thus a multiple virtual device capable of replacing actual physical devices as envisioned. It thus has power to disrupt established industries like PC, TV, laptop and wireless handset manufacturers with major economic and business impacts. Although such disruption is beneficial to consumers, it will have negative effects on the established incumbents.

We are now at the beginning of constructing actionable cyberspaces where we can measure any pertinent attributes of corresponding physical spaces on this planet by sensor swarms and webs and act autonomously to manipulate these physical spaces as per our desires. We are essentially de-territorializing the physical space through actionable cyberspace where actions in cyberspace are conveyed to corresponding physical space actions. This actionable cyberspace is making all of us as immigrants in this world where we can work and act in any place we choose, with no territorial jurisdictions and geographic boundaries. We can catalog people, process delocalized streams of data and anonymously exercise power over people and their surroundings with incalculable consequences. We can use that power for the benefit of our businesses to offer many people high velocity services such as providing health and welfare services, emergency services, precision agricultural services, and many other internal and external business services. How will we build and implement such actionable cyberspace? We must consider its de-territorialization effects by considering protection of proprietary property rights, personal rights and privacy considerations with the following attributes:

- It must be an instrument to promote the development of human services to accommodate health and welfare, emergency and danger prevention with alerts and proper physical actions, education and training, leisure and entertainment services, shopping transactions and banking services, and the like.
- It must accommodate diversity and integrate various services geared towards individuals rather than to masses of people as in mass media.

- It must be able to make use of the large streams of data flowing across networks, and their accumulated knowledge and messages to exploit the collective knowledge of humans.
- It must be able to operate remotely, autonomously and in real-time to manipulate physical spaces as well as personal spaces like human bodies, animal bodies, and various industrial and agricultural machinery and associated processes.

Implementation and use of such a actionable cyberspace system will have two major effects on our work and culture:

1. It will blur the differences between designers, producers, implementers, creators, authors and users, each helping to sustain the activity of others by dissolving their identities.
2. Information, messages, sensor observation of things and places, sensor data and action-oriented commands are all geared toward individual businesses. Representation is now subject to sampling, combining, reusing and modifying actionable messages as per the context, either programmatically and autonomously or manually, which will greatly diminish human efforts to attain high velocity specified results.

Wireless mobility is essentially electronic mobility at the speed of light. It offers enormous benefits to businesses and enterprises. It compresses time several fold, resulting in high velocity business operations and at the same time expanding the geographical reach of business enormously all over the world. Importantly, it enables real-time business processes and many proactive faster-than-real-time business processes. Faster-than-real-time business operations and processes require predictive analytics with prescriptive analytics requiring real-time data and frequently high-speed streaming data inputs. Even simple anticipatory process models with high-speed-streaming data provide powerful faster-than real-time operations to provide significant competitive advantages and new business opportunities that are not known in the current state of the art.

Furthermore, wireless mobility provides attractive new ways of offering business services like mobile control of machinery, mobile banking, mobile insurance services, mobile healthcare services and the like by employing rich sensors available on mobile smartphone devices. The fundamental building blocks of such a mobile business enterprise are mobile platforms, wireless devices like smartphones and mobile apps.

Wireless business constituents are wireless devices like smartphones, wireless and wired networks, smartphone apps and their associated platforms.

Smartphone platforms and enterprise mobile forms are the essential pillars on which wireless mobile enterprise stands.

Speed is essential to survive and thrive for any business. In nature, a fast-acting predator can get its meal and similarly, fast-acting prey can escape the danger. In business, speed also wins. Fast-acting businesses have enormous advantages over their competitors.

High velocity business processes significantly increase the value of any business. Business success depends on quick response to changing customer desires, the rapidly changing marketplace and competition. Electronic mobility offers such fast response to the needs of all stakeholders of the business.

The DNA of mobile business is **Devices**, **Network** and **Apps**. The technologies of Devices of smartphones and tablets, Networks of 4G, 5G and other advanced mobile networks and Apps of the smartphones have advanced by leaps and bounds, and they offer huge opportunities to any business to take advantage of high-speed electronic mobility.

Electronic mobility with smartphones and other wireless devices provides a business with not only high-speed but also rich-sensor capabilities to contextualize many business processes through predictive modeling and anticipatory actions to conduct many business processes faster than real-time. It provides not only high efficiency, but also intelligent business processes to conduct new effective and faster ways to out-compete and out-do the established incumbents. Several new businesses have already blossomed – Instagram, Pinterest, Facebook, Airbnb and Uber – based on smartphones and electronic mobility.

Electronic mobility has already captured every aspect of our life from how we transact with businesses to how we communicate with each other to how we educate and entertain. Electronic mobility enables high-speed business processes and transactions with extended reach and with more efficiency to all stakeholders, such as workers, customers, partners and suppliers. It offers high compression of time and space, resulting in orders-of-magnitude business efficiencies.

Electronic mobility provides deeper insights into all business operations with contextual sensor data analysis and fusion, as provided by smartphones. It enables the business to realize the following examples through deeper insights and big data analytics for better decisions:

- Faster-than-real-time business operations by making use of predictive modeling and anticipatory determination of business tasks with contextual situation analysis based on processing of high-speed streaming data in real-time and from other data sources.

- Perpetual customer engagement at a fraction of the cost for superior customer relations.
- 24-hour, 365-day monitoring and acting on many mission-critical tasks; for example, when attending patients with critical illnesses and taking care of other patients with insignificant costs and expenditures due to wearable wireless sensors.

Current mobile platforms are primarily built upon smartphone operating systems. These mobile platforms are well matured for individual consumer applications, but their applications to business and enterprise are still evolving. Businesses that have mastered best utilizing the electronic high mobility – like Uber, WhatsApp, Facebook, Amazon, Google and some others – have radically transformed the traditional industry landscape. Thus, this Element focuses on business and enterprise applications based on mobile platforms.

Just as the Internet and the Web changed our world and business, electronic mobility is changing our lives and work. Mobility at electronic speeds plays a crucial role in every aspect of business and in all categories of businesses. It invariably brings immense business transformations that are often disruptive, as in the case of recent entrants like Uber, Airbnb, Facebook, Twitter, Instagram, Waze, Pinterest, Foursquare, Zynga and several more. For established enterprises and businesses, it offers unprecedented efficiencies, expansions and new ways of conducting business with superior competitive advantage.

The value of electronic mobility in any business increases exponentially by using multiple business applications and multiple sources of data, some in real-time and some in databases such as those available from government databases like census, weather, satellite, GPS and business stats and from several private sources like Google, Facebook, Twitter and Waze.

1.4 Disruptive Industry Changes with Multiple Apps and Multiple Databases

Many of the data sources referred to are not only free but they also provide real-time content. Because of the importance of such digital disruptive changes, we will deal these topics in detail later in the Element.

Even a single mobile business application is useful, but single application is very common and trivial. Businesses that quickly make use of mobility combined with myriad different data sources interacting with each other in on-line and off-line modes with smartphone users are truly disruptive and they reap benefits over others. Wireless sensor data, social networks, superior analytics, algorithms and cloud computing complement electronic mobility and, as such, they pave the way for radical breakthroughs in the marketplace. Such applications result in nonlinear effects at many levels that are hard to understand. Thus, one of the objectives of this Element is to understand the impact of mobility applications and benefits in a more fundamental way.

Our business and enterprise environments have already undergone immense transformation triggered by smartphone electronic mobility which is like the previous Internet revolution. We are witnessing this transformation all around us. Everywhere in our daily lives – from how we transact with businesses, how we work and educate, and how we entertain – are things based on the smartphone. Mobile phones are now exceeding 8 billion, which is about the world population. The average person has a smart phone and looks at it in excess of 100 times per day, that is every 15 minutes or so for text messages, phone calls, emails, time and calendar services, and so on. Furthermore, the market for wireless wearables is growing exponentially each year, which is propelling electronic mobility to a new level.

The importance of work location is significantly reduced and even made irrelevant in many business processes. Mobility offers high flexibility and new forms of conducting work across organizational boundaries with new effective ways of collaborating with workers, customers and other stakeholders, as well as dealing with objects and machines.

2 Makeup of High Velocity Enterprise

Making a high velocity enterprise consists of introducing high velocity business operations with high mobility across all business tasks. The strategic aspects of high velocity enterprise are well covered in MIT professor Steven J. Spear's 2015 book. In this Element, we deal with how to formulate and achieve high velocity business operations that are essential to making a high velocity enterprise.

The smartphone has dominated enterprise and our lives with its built-in computing and communications capabilities along with its immense sensory powers, like cameras, GPS, accelerometer, altimeter, gyro, sound and other sensors, and its powerful multi-core computing capabilities. Its ease of use with natural user interfaces, wide availability at any place and at any time and affordable consumer price is driving its use in many enterprise business processes. We are beginning to witness the replacement of PCs with smartphones for many business and professional applications, potentially moving toward the high velocity real-time enterprise era where smartphones are ideal due to their immense sensors accessibility and their ability to offer virtual workspace and dashboards on the screen. The current workhorses of desktop and laptop PCs are becoming less relevant.

High velocity business operations in an enterprise have major benefits when high connectivity between data and processes takes place, as in these examples:

- When point-of-sale data is employed with manufacturing and stored warehouse data, the business can efficiently optimize its supply chain to increase sales and to provide world-class customer experience.
- A business can predict when its machinery or a piece of equipment might fail by spotting defects in production line, resulting in preventive actions with significant saving of expenses.
- A freight operation can reroute during busy congestion times, thus improving customer efficiency and savings.

Achieving similar benefits with up-to-date real-time information will become normal to the enterprise when proper mobile devices and platforms are employed as described in the succeeding sections of this Element.

2.1 Prevalent PC versus Smartphone

Mobile computing devices like smartphones are only slowly finding business applications and they have not yet replaced PCs and laptops in any significant way. PCs are still the workhorses of the business and enterprise and this situation may continue for few years. Soon, however, smartphones will start to replace PCs and laptops in a measurable way because of their wide availability, low cost, ease of operation and millions of apps that are already available on them. As an end user computing device, the smartphone has advantages over PC for work-related tasks, as shown in Table1.

As seen from Table 1, a smartphone provides many different user experiences far different and superior to those of the PC, making it a preferred work tool replacing the conventional PC desktop.

2.2 Work and Workplace Transformation

Electronic mobility has changed the prior legacy concepts of work and workplace. The concept of work as performed at a workplace generally located in a fixed geographic location of a business is becoming less relevant.

- Electronic mobility transforms work as a fluid and global collaborative item that can be performed at any place and at any time.
- It interacts with all business stakeholders – employees, employers, customers, suppliers, partners and others – in a continuous uninterrupted manner, thus providing better coordination and work efficiency as well as increased velocity.

Table 1 Conventional PC versus smartphone advantages

No.	Item	PC-Desktop /Laptop	Smartphone	Comparative impact
1	Access and availability	At a desk	Any place and time	Immensely better
2	Application programs available	Few hundred thousand with bulky codes	Millions of "apps" with light code	Order of magnitude more mobile apps versus PC applications
3	Mapping and selecting	Mouse and touchpad clicks	Natural gesture navigation	20 seconds versus 2 seconds
4	Data capture	Keyboard data entry	NFC, bar code and QR codes automatically captured	40 seconds versus sub-second
5	Capturing location, address and relevant environment details	Manual keyboard entry	GPS aided lookup, automatic and often real-time	Immensely superior
6	Image capture	Manual and tedious	Built-in camera	Immensely superior
7	Accelerometer for movement input	Not available	Built-in and automatic	Immensely superior
8	Various sensors data inputs like direction, temperature, pressure and the like	Not available	Automatic	Immensely superior

Increasing proliferation of electronic mobility in business is inevitable due to the following powerful drivers:

- Business efficiency and extending electronic mobility across time and space,
- Proliferation of inexpensive and free databases, like government census, health and income, and social network data, which aid in structuring new value-creation frameworks for superior business services,
- Global competition demanding fast services and responses,

- Readily available and mature smartphones with powerful computing and networking capabilities at consumer affordable costs,
- Increasing numbers of Millennials between 15 and 35 years entering the business arena, and
- Cloud technologies encompassing 4G and 5G broadband fabric, social networks', real-time data and analytics, virtualized processes and resources and the like. This will aid in creating superior collaborative systems that can replace traditional transaction methods, offering knowledge and insights to the right people regarding the right context and objects.

Two other fundamental forces for inevitable mobile business proliferation are:

- Explosion of mobile devices with more power at throwaway consumer prices, and
- Explosion of digital data which is readily available.

Apart from these drivers and forces, businesses want to shift their professional and skilled tasks to locations where talent is readily available at lower costs to improve operational performance. This is already taking place in knowledge-intensive businesses like healthcare, information services, and content and media production, where regional expertise blossomed worldwide at a very low cost compared to the prevailing static workforce. Driven by mobile cloud platforms of networked collaboration, virtual workers and teams can apply expert skills both internally and externally for the benefit of the enterprise. Social networking and social databases, along with several real-time sensor databases of public and private domains, are not only replacing traditional enterprise structures but extending them to deliver enterprise offerings in real-time, and in some instances faster-than-real-time, with the help of contextual situation analysis and advanced analytics.

2.3 Challenges Facing High Velocity Business Mobility

There are major challenges facing a company trying to introduce electronic mobility in its business operations to meet the expectations of mobile employees and other stakeholders – customers, partners, suppliers and administrators – while dealing with security, high costs, ever-changing technologies and a proliferation of wireless devices, apps and systems. Challenges include:

- Inclusion of a variety of wireless devices entering the market and deploying them with proper configurations and apps;
- Limited wireless bandwidth along with frequent network interruptions;

- Accomplishing wide interoperability to a growing array of devices, wireless network providers, maintenance and support; and
- Adequate security to ensure lost or stolen mobile devices, unauthorized access and making business data secure.

Since high velocity and mobile business is still evolving, there are no established standards, benchmarks and best practices. Therefore, an implementer faces formidable problems compounded by exponential numbers of devices, systems proliferation and rapidly changing technologies. However, the recently emerging technologies and standards of IoT and 5G provide some guidance.

Often an implementer requires a customized interactive platform to offer anyone, anywhere, anytime relevant connectivity and access to business processes like ERP (Enterprise Resource Planning), CRM (Customer Relation Management), SCM (Supplier Chain Management) and other back-end resources for remote persons. Essentially, any worker should be able to access real-time business information (such as those of ERP, SCM and the like), and other pertinent external data resources like Google, Facebook, national government–provided data sources and those offered by international bodies like the UN, World Bank, ITU (International Telecommunications Union), and UNESCO.

2.4 High Velocity Business Foundation

High velocity business is centered on mobile business. It is founded on wireless data network cloud infrastructure supported by real-time data accessible to any worker on any device at any time as shown in the Figure 1.

The real-time available data from internal and external sources are processed programmatically by mobile device apps, application programming interfaces (APIs) and analytics for the desired business operation. These resources are

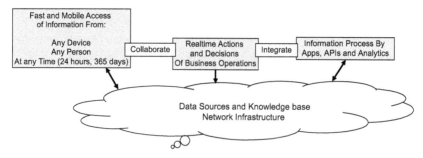

Figure 1 Makeup of high velocity business operations

generally accessed from network infrastructure that connects external and internal databases through cloud computing.

The three most important ingredients required to perform a chosen business operation are appropriately selected (or developed) apps, APIs and analytics as shown in the right-hand side of Figure 1.

Apps are mobile phone applications designed for doing a few purposeful things with very little footprint in contrast to conventional bulky applications designed for PCs to do many things with several features. Traditional business PC and server applications like CRM and ERP are very expensive and need professional workers to configure and apply them. In contrast, mobile apps are simple to use and can be downloaded from App stores for immediate use. Apps are developed on mobile platforms of smartphones and they can be developed rapidly with the tools available on the platforms. Applications are developed on different IDEs (integrated development environments) with elaborate software design processes.

APIs are compared to application programming interfaces of the past, but in the modern view they should be considered products to be consumed by users (although they are made with software code). An API exposes a business capability to external users which the user desires. It is a way of engaging the user for a given business, augmented by Facebook, Twitter, Pinterest and other businesses from their respective APIs. Some popular APIs are Google Maps API to enable a developer to embed Google Maps on a webpage using JavaScript or Flash interface; YouTube APIs to enable developers to integrate YouTube videos into their websites; YouTube Analytics API, YouTube Streaming API etc. Many APIs are offered by cloud providers like Microsoft and Amazon, and can be customized for a specific business operation. Similarly, APIs of internal business programs like SAP, CRM and other business-specific programs will be useful in accomplishing desired business operations.

3 Mobile Aspects of High Velocity Business Operations

Many businesses operate at fixed locations, such as business premises. In order to attain high velocity, as well as de-territorialization of business, it is important to convert business operations to mobile work operations, as we will discuss later in this Element.

Electronic mobility has already affected many aspects of personal and professional life. GPS monitoring of our driving habits and insurance safe-driver discounts are one such example. Similarly, it is now starting to take over many business operations. Figure 2 shows that core business operations, such as

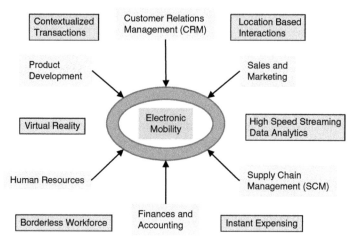

Figure 2 Examples of electronic mobility in enterprise business

product development, customer relation management, sales and marketing, supply-chain management (SCM), finance accounting and human resources, provide opportunities to introduce several high velocity business operations.

Many applications of electronic mobility include acquiring contextual sensor data along with relevant public and private data available through governments and social network sites like Twitter and Facebook. Therefore apps, APIs and high-speed data analytics that frequently involve real-time high-speed streaming data analytics as well as anonymized public and private data play an important role.

Electronic mobility offers many benefits to a business. Listed individually, they seem obvious, but as a categorized comprehensive pool, such as we provide here, they can enable the reader to apply electronic mobility for maximum benefit to his/her business.

3.1 Benefits of Electronic Mobility

In order to fully reap the benefits of electronic mobility, a business must possess or develop an underlying infrastructure based on the following items. We deal with them in detail in the later parts of the Element:

- Utilize cloud-based architecture to serve a stakeholder/customer at any place and at any time;
- Provide relevant business services to stakeholders with any mobile device they use; and
- Develop and enable big data–based solutions to

o Analyze streaming high speed and stationary data for real-time and faster-than-real-time service provisioning. Faster-than-real-time service provisioning requires stakeholder and environmental contextualization and predictive real-time analysis of one or more streams of data.

o Quickly adapt to the changing and evolving stakeholder requirements; and

o Create a single view of the stakeholder across the business.

Speed-Related Benefits: Work requires specific resources to be brought to the workplace. Electronic mobility speeds up bringing in resources spread across many locations at the right time and the right place. It involves ensuring proper contact, communication and coordination in obtaining such resources. This involves subtasks like enquiries, authorizations, payments, shipping and multi-party acceptance. A smartphone with properly prompted screens and with few touches and clicks can accomplish all these subtasks and others more quickly than traditional paper-based processes like purchase orders, payments and others. Electronic mobility not only speeds but coordinates getting required resources, even acting as work-performance aids with proper screen prompts and menus.

Coordination and Synchronization: Mobility offers real-time coordination of resources to deliver at a specific location at a specific time as well as coordinating workers and synchronizing the work to the task at hand. Businesses reap significant benefits from such real-time coordination and synchronization of resources and workers. In traditional paper-based businesses such coordination is delayed and tedious. Thus, jobs that were done in weeks and days with legacy paper-based processes can now be done in few minutes with simple easy touches on a screen.

Information Aspects: Information logistics is essential for a business to thrive and compete. It involves collection of information from various external and internal databases, transmission, analysis, reporting, sharing and taking actions. The faster and more efficient such collection, analysis and action, the more competitive the business. Electronic mobility and cloud computing provide tools for this.

Time and Space Compression: Mobile applications provide a means to extend business from a single location to many distant geographical locations, compressing distance without adding additional premises, labor, assets, inventories and other resources.

Similarly, these applications speed up business processes thus compressing the time necessary to do the work. Examples include identifying digital online markets, identifying prospects, customizing products and services to individual prospects and delivering required services and products at right time at right location.

Real-Time Sensor Data Applications: Smartphones with several internal sensors, as well as their capacity to interface with a host of many external sensors and sensor networks through their built-in Bluetooth and Wi-Fi capabilities, provide real-time contextual data for fast and accurate decision-making.

Business Multiplier Effects: Multiplier effects increase the effectiveness of a person, business process or item, separately, or in combination. With a smartphone and electronic mobility, a small team can work with suppliers, producers and customers spread across continents through simple email, texting, voice, Skype, Google+ etc., along with cloud-based apps or spreadsheets from anywhere, even while traveling in a car or airplane. Therefore, productivity increases significantly.

3.2 Mobility Basics

Mobility is broadly considered a metaphor of global fluids, the heterogeneous, uneven and unpredictable mobilities of people, information, objects, money, images and risks, that move quickly and chaotically across regions with their deterritorialized aspects (Mol and Law, 1994). People and businesses that take advantage of mobility technologies can become geographically independent.

Mobility is defined in the dictionary as ability to move or capacity to change place. Mobile is a state and is defined as "capable of movement; characterized by facility of movement." Recently, mobility has assumed importance in business and in life as increased deployment of smartphones compresses time and space.

Mobile and mobility are popular words used in many disciplines and in many different contexts. For example, these words apply to physical and nonphysical entities like people, objects, intangible objects, money and work. In terms of smartphone use, we must rethink mobility as a metaphor in an interconnected fabric of humans, information and tangible and intangible objects that flow within and across territorial boundaries at a moment's notice.

Mobility fundamentally alters the way entities interact. Mobility is defined by its three-dimensional attributes: time, space and context. These three attributes are basic in any mobility transformation, as in human interaction.

Mobility changes space (i.e. location). This dimension is familiar to us and space and time are intertwined in a fundamental way. Human mobility along space and time is important in all businesses. Similarly, mobility of intangible objects, for example, the movement of information through various channels like the Internet, satellite, wireless 4G, 5G, Wi-Fi, TV and radio signals, plays a major role in all aspects of human life. The context dimension of mobility refers to the situation and environment wherein people perform their activities. This dimension of mobility is less understood, and we will deal with it later.

Castells's (1996) seminal works on the "space of flows and timeless time" are relevant to current mobile businesses since they provide fundamental basics in conceptualizing and developing real-time businesses that respond and operate at the speed of light. Since real-time businesses operate at the highest theoretically possible speed of light, one can wonder at the ultimate achievement in speed of business. But faster than speed of light business operations are certainly possible and such operations are vital to compete in the current marketplace. Such operations are possible thanks to contextual analysis of scores of streaming data from various sensors in smartphones and other sensor networks and acting in advance of real-time by anticipating changing business needs and customer requirements. Castells also dealt with the role of context in the space of flows and placeless space (such as cyber space). We briefly describe these concepts as pertinent to high velocity business operations.

Space and time are fundamental and universal attributes of our lives and the universe, but space alone cannot exist, and it is not defined even in physics. Space exists only with reference to material objects at a point in time. It is defined only with its attributes of material objects and time. Our businesses and lives exist around space of flows: flows of money, objects, information, senses of sound, video and their representations, flows of organizational interactions and the like. It is essential to note the enormous impact of the new breed of mobile wireless devices like smartphones in shaping space and the space of flows.

We can better grasp and define the space of flows of our mobile information age by looking at the detailed descriptions in Castells's writings as summarized herein. The space of flows comprises flows of various materials facilitated by the underlying network of infrastructure. This infrastructure has three layers.

The **first layer** is the material support allowing the flow of electronic impulses through, for example, terrestrial fiber-optic links and 4G, 5G, satellite, TV and other channels. The first layer can be compared to the industrial era's roads, railroads, and airways.

The **second layer** illustrates that space of flows is not placeless, but it has specific places of exchanges and communication hubs playing the role of coordination and routing. Hubs and nodes are hierarchically placed; they are akin to towns and cities. Global cities like London, Paris and New York are examples to illustrate the place-based aspect of space of flows where capital flows.

The **third layer** of the space of flows relates to the spatial organization of the dominant executive elites who configure and reconfigure the space around them. This aspect as articulated by Castells deals with human social organization and how cities and regions develop. It is also directly relevant to the businesses that exist under these space flows.

We are always immersed in time. Time is inextricably linked to space of flows. According to Castells, in nature, as in society, all time is specific to a given context. Time is essentially a local concept linked to the context. Businesses and our activities are by and large associated with mechanical "clock time." In this mobile smartphone age, "time–space compression" is everywhere, as is especially evident by working in real-time and even working faster than real-time.

The concept of virtual time has emerged in the modern networked society and businesses where instantaneous information is constantly transmitted across the globe, acquired through news reporters and information from sensors and computer databases on dynamic business data as well as technical data. Virtual time can be mixed with real time to create a temporal collage where past, present and future are mixed to suit to the needs of business and society.

The aspect of timelessness of time is discussed by Castells (1996) as it takes place when the characteristics of a given context, namely the informational paradigm and the network society, impart systemic perturbation in the sequential order of phenomena performed in that context. This perturbation is responsible for time-space compression, real-time business operations and in scheming faster-than-real-time operations. It introduces random discontinuity in the sequence and creation of undifferentiated time.

We consider mobility as applied to the three entities: 1. humans, 2. information and 3. objects. These entities play a crucial role in businesses and in our lives and most business tasks involve the mobility of them.

3.3 Mobility of Humans

Humans move around to perform their daily work and activities. Modern mobile workers do not work in a formal office, but at different places in a boundary-less environment. The mobilities associated with a mobile person are classified into three categories as per Kristofferson and Ljungberg (2000): 1. travelling, 2. visiting and 3. wandering.

Travel is the act of going from one place to another via walking, bus, air and the like. Visiting is an act of spending time or visiting a place to meet someone on purpose. Visiting involves transitory time. Wandering is a process involving extensive mobility in and around local premises. Wandering is common in a business premise where many personnel wander in a local area during their work time.

The current crop of mobile devices – smartphones, tablets, some laptops – are eminently suited to these three types of mobility to perform many business tasks. However, the smartphone has a better edge due to its size, sensor capabilities and wide communication capabilities.

3.4 Mobility of Information

Our business and lives are based on the flows of several entities: flows of money, flows of information, flows of technologies, flows of images sounds and symbols, flows of business interactions and flows of objects. Information flow is a basic attribute to these entities. In business, information about customers, facilities and resources, and their changes and dynamics, plays a vital role.

Information flow through various channels like satellite, internet and communication networks, is the backbone of the modern life and business. Relentless flow of information and its mobility to convey visual images, sounds and data occurs at an increasing rate where information embodies a critical part of business and social conditions.

With the touch of an application icon, many financial transactions, such as payments and transfer of funds and capital across the globe, can be consummated at electronic speed. Here, physical money is not moved, but only digital codes representing the money and transaction information. Such electronic transactions and transfer of money and capital has enormous benefits and cost advantages over the past paper-based transactions.

A vast quantity of images, sounds and symbols are transferred and transacted through hybrid terrestrial and mobile networks and webs. Such transfers dematerialize communications between billions of persons and bring forth virtual special businesses and communities. Physical space is abstracted into ever-increasing cyberspace where distance and territorial jurisdictions and national boundaries are made irrelevant. Such transfers are the backbone to reaping enormous cost advantages and speed of business processes.

3.5 Mobility of Objects

Movement of objects happens daily, such as sending and receiving parcels, freight and mail by some means of transportation. Global mobility of parts and components in making many modern articles like electronic items like smartphones and mechanical items like airplanes and automobiles is increasing happening and allowing businesses to be competitive.

In many instances, the movement of objects is closely associated with the movement of people. Personal objects like mobile phones and wireless wearables move along with humans and their movement is intimately intertwined with human mobility. Many objects, like recent mobile wearables, are an extension of the human body itself and are part of the required equipment of the contemporary nomad. The common wallet, watch and shoes are evolving into smart wireless wearables providing immense convenience and benefits.

Mobile field workers like salespersons, customer-equipment repairpersons and field healthcare professionals, carry everyday mobile objects like tablets, smartphones and other mobile equipment as appropriate to their work. In order to best develop such mobile equipment and associated apps, it is important to consider mobile interactions. We deal with such mobile interactions in some detail the following sections.

4 Nature of Mobile Work

Mobile work is an integral part of high velocity business operations. Prevailing business operations largely depend on fixed-premises workplaces and paper-based processes such as work-order approvals, authorization of worker schedules and several other invoicing and payment operations that are slow and often hindered by manual coordination and approvals. They are unsuited to high velocity operations. Converting such business operations into mobile work operations allow them to be performed in high velocity operations.

The concept of mobile work "at any time and at any place," as often envisioned, is not practical in many businesses. Most businesses have tasks to be performed within certain time periods, as well as in certain locations with certain human–object interactions. Some tasks involve human supervision and administrative approvals.

Success of mobile business depends on finding successful mobile services and mobile interactions. It is important to note that mobile work is distinctly different from immobile work. It is not the same as using mobile communications and information technologies in daily work routines that are primarily based on communications.

Static routine mobile work is already implemented in many businesses and many of its applications tend to be simple. In a general case of mobile work, it is necessary to consider mobile workers and their mobile interactions as they transform within a network of human and non-human entities, and outcomes of the mobile work on administrative and managerial actions. Special attention should be placed to mobile workers' capacity to manage mobile interactions, interaction management in a given context and factors affecting the success of mobile interaction in a given business context.

In evaluating the success and effectiveness of mobile work usability in a business task, there are metrics that can be applied. The primary effectiveness is, of course, a business productivity increase. These metrics are shown in Table 2, partly derived from the works of Hurkmans and Van Elsen (2012).

It is important to note that weight factors must be assigned to individual business tasks depending on their contexts. In health and safety industries, errors are intolerable due to life-and-death situations, and hence error tolerance should be very high even compared to efficiency. In leisure and entertainment contexts, efficiency is more important than error tolerance. Error metrics involve the number of errors, ability to recover from errors and existence of serious errors. Error prevention, by making the user avoid errors with repeated tests or in other ways, is also a factor.

ISO 9241, an international human computer standard, places emphasis on items 1, 2 and 6 of Table 2 and many professionals have used these three items in their usability studies. Item 3 of the table is equally important, since in many mission-critical tasks errors have catastrophic consequences, for example, in healthcare, first-responder tasks and the like. In such tasks, item 3 must be more heavily weighted than items 1, 2 and 6.

Table 2 Mobile work evaluation metrics

No.	Measure	Typical example of weight factor assignment
1	Efficiency	32
2	Effectiveness	30
3	Errors	25
4	Attitude	8
5	Ease of Learning	8
6	Satisfaction	5
7	Accessibility	5
8	Operability	4
9	Memorability	3
10	Acceptability	3
11	Flexibility	3

4.1 Work Transformation with Mobile Interactions

It is important to focus on the work outcome of a mobile interaction with a mobile worker and the associated interactions within a network of human and nonhuman entities. Modeling of mobile work provides a greater understanding of how we can manage mobile interactions in a given business context and what factors we should consider in successful implementation of mobile interactions.

Mobile work and mobile virtual work have many facets and they are dealt with in a book by Andriessen et al. (2006). Mobile work contains mobile virtual work, mobile workers and mobile technologies where workers and workplaces change. New concepts of mobile places and spaces, and virtual workplace have been introduced in the Andriessen et al. reference. Here, a basic tripartite – subject-tool-object – is the basic functional unit of mobile work, which is performed as actions in different working contexts or spaces.

Mobile work commonly refers to a task that can be completed "anywhere at any time" by employing mobile technologies. It refers to mobile places and spaces with reference to working contexts, moving subjects and objects using mobile tools along with the ability of a worker to move around. It is extended to the perspectives of the purposes of a mobile worker in 1. physical spaces, 2. virtual spaces and 3. mental and social spaces as in Table 3, as per contributions made in Vainio et al. (2008).

In the previous section, we referred the three modes of mobility in humans: visiting, wandering and traveling. In addition to these physical geographical movements, mobile work includes operational and interactional mobility. Interactional mobility means intense and fluid interaction with a wide range of staff associated with the work. The characteristics of mobile work include how its task is structured, its frequency and the geographical location where the worker typically performs the task. The mobile worker is often involved in actions other than information processing and communications and handles

Table 3 Mobile workspaces and purposes

No.	Space	Purposes of activities
1	Physical space	Defines physical space with distances, settings and physical environments
2	Virtual space	Electronic display presentation, connections, devices and applications
3	Mental and social spaces	Shared common experiences

multiple tasks. Mobile workers have different roles to play and the task can be structured or non-structured, with differing frequencies and locations. Other variables include differing mobile contexts and mobile technologies.

Physical mobile interactions comprise communication between objects, mobile user, mobile device and other objects of the physical world, and in cyberspace with a touch screen, touch pad, mouse, electronic pen and speech inputs. Physical mobile interactions from device to device have been developed by several technologies like Bluetooth, Wi-Fi, near field communication (NFC), radio frequency identification (RFID chips) and other innovative technologies. As an example, a user can simply point their mobile device with an embedded camera at a distant object, like a poster or an advertising board of a public place, at a marker (generally barcode). Such an interaction can be programmed to trigger a web-page display or other actions. Another mode of interaction is through a user's mobile device remotely triggering interaction with another mobile device which can further act on objects, places and other people as selected for specified actions and results.

Context is the most important element in developing proper interactions for mobile apps as they differ significantly from traditional PC-desktop and server applications because of severe constraints and disruptions caused by mobility. In general, are caused by mobility issues such as unfavorable noise and light conditions, fluctuating environmental conditions, vastly varying attention levels and the like due to travel, airport waiting, meetings etc. We provide here basic guidelines to aid the mobile app designer to better design mobile apps to suit to specified business tasks.

Mobile interactions are personal, user driven, and specific to the mobile device at hand. New ways of conveying information through vibrations, changing temperature, blinking and/or fading display of video signals, virtual presence and other ambient indicators will greatly aid the interactions. Such interactions should only overlay without interrupting any critical ongoing activities.

- Ease of use in the mobile context is essential, despite noise and distractions.
- The current crop of mobile devices offers continuous companionship with an always-on feature. Such devices should be able to take multiple interactions within a day with infrequent interruptions of routine activities.
- Mobile interactions should be capable of extending beyond the devicem such as activating sensor actuators by mere pointing or other simple interfaces.

Mobile interaction design is a new emerging field and mobile apps should consider contexts and must be customized to meet relevant contexts as

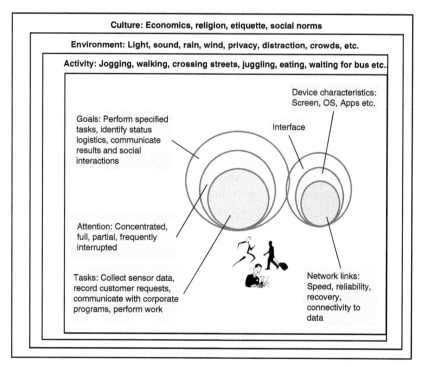

Figure 3 Depiction of mobile contexts to consider

depicted in Figure 3; for details refer to (Nadav Savio). In Figure 3, goals are emphasized at two levels to denote working party and receiving party, while attention and tasks are relegated to inner layers common to all. It is important to note such mobile interactions eliminate paper-based business operations and put them in the electronic domain for enabling high velocity business operations.

As shown in the Figure 3, goals must be specified for tasks by identifying real-time status and communicating them to the designated parties. In the mobile environment, attention is frequently interrupted by external conditions and events and this should be mitigated.

4.2 Mobile Work Networks and Modeling

Mobile work eliminates slow paper-based operations like worker approvals and scheduling documents with proper management approvals that delay business considerably. Hence, it is essential to formulate and model mobile work accordingly to reduce and eliminate slow paper-based operations as well to smooth the flow of instantaneous interactions between humans. This process enables attainment of high velocity business operations.

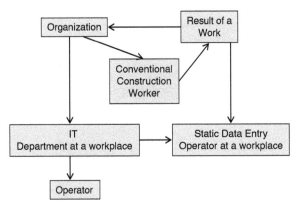

Figure 4 Example of a simple construction worker work map

Initial physical work models should be made with detailed steps. Various techniques of such modeling methodologies are already prevalent under the names of flow-charting, UML (Unified Modeling Language) models, BPM (Business Process Model), P-graphs and the like. These topics are dealt extensively in the literature (for example, Sharp et al., 2012; Damelio 2011). Physical work models can be converted to mobile work models, by extending them.

We will briefly consider work mapping, called MoBis Map, as developed in Vainio et al. (2008), which is based on an improvement of the previous ANT (Actor Network Theory). We illustrate a construction worker example of safety measurement process by two simple examples based on this reference. The first example, Figure 4, shows work without mobile service and in the second example mobile service is introduced to show how work is transformed. Mobile work causes instantaneous conditions and augments the ordinary work with mobile interactions to hasten it. This transformation of work due to mobile services in the contexts of mobile work is important to consider in formulating superior mobile work for high velocity business operations.

In Figure 4, we have modeled worker interactions as a network map without mobile service, to show the construction worker's safety measurement process. The worker directly interacts with his organization and supervisors as per organization policies for the work he is performing, and indirectly with a data entry worker. Introduction of mobile service changes this work map and the interactions between different actors are shown in Figure 5.

In Figure 5, we introduced mobile service for the construction worker to carry out his safety measurement task. Here the construction worker is directly connected not only to his organization and supervisors but also to a corporate data center, mobile service provider, mobile device and mobile operator. In

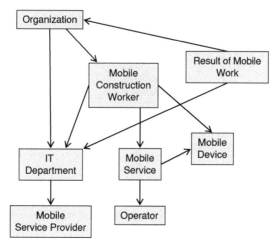

Figure 5 Mapping of work with mobile service

developing this MoBis Map analysis of transformation due to mobile services, the following steps are proposed:

- Determine the principal actor (in this case the construction worker);
- Specify and define the important principal actors in the current contexts which are human and non-human;
- Focus on the critical actors;
- Determine how the actors' network is changed or not due to mobility services;
- Analyze transformations due to interactions; and
- Define the influences of the transformation on mobile work.

In this example, we have only considered a simple case of routine work. MoBis-map method applies to many cases of mobile work formulation that are more complex, where different actors both human and nonhuman act in various ways. Such mobile work formulation and implementation makes up high velocity business operations for higher efficiencies.

In Figure 6, we illustrate a range of mobile works starting from routine to nonroutine based on total mobility as in Taxi Driver to Multi Mobility of a typical Salesman to Micro Mobility as per Virtual Teams.

5 Conventional-Work to Mobile-Work Conversion

Humans want to be increasingly mobile to increase their opportunities. They move around their homes and offices, wander in convention centers, wander around city centers and streets and travel in cars and airplanes. Such mobility

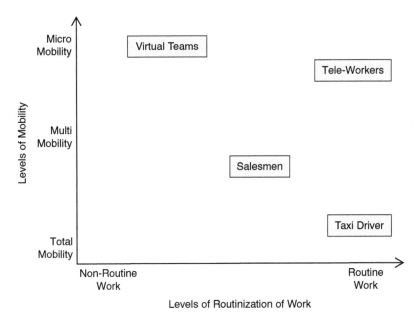

Figure 6 Types of mobile work

offers opportunities and also inconveniences by disconnecting people from their familiar surroundings both in immediate proximity and nearby places. Mobile work thus includes disruptions to the availability of resources such as information, work facilities and colleagues. However, such disruptions are compensated for by the modern mobile work technologies of smartphones and apps that are reconnecting people to remote work facilities, other people and other resources. It is important to note that any work involves a mobile component and a stationary component. The degree of mobility varies from one job category to another.

In Table 4 we provide typical mobility profiles of current workers based on author experience. It is important to note that these mobility profiles are changing rapidly and increasing due to advances in mobile devices and commoditization of smartphones, and due to increased enterprise mobility. We believe that future workers' profiles will change drastically toward more mobile knowledge workers, professionals and specialists. We have already witnessed that many past job categories like blue-collar workers, secretaries and certain agricultural labor jobs have almost declined to extinction.

We provide a simple example of how paper-based work will be transformed by mobile work processes. Later we discuss many back-end processes and their architectures for more detailed mobile work formulations. Figure 7 illustrates

Table 4 Typical mobility profiles of worker categories of current era

	On premises		Outside	
Category	**At desk**	**Away**	**At desk**	**On the Road**
Designer/Developer	85%	15%		
Manager or Supervisor	65%	35%		
Maintenance worker	15%	85%		
Tele Worker			100%	
Consultant			20%	80%
Sales Executive			10%	90%
Entrepreneur/CEO	20%	20%	30%	30%
Specialist/Knowledge worker	10%	40%	10%	40%

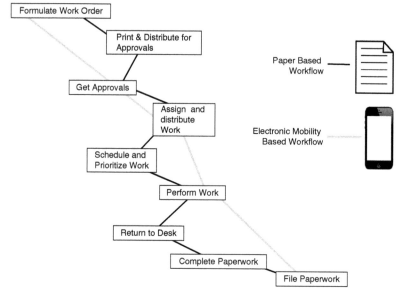

Figure 7 Paper-based work to mobile work transformation

a way of accomplishing high velocity business operation through yellow line paths rather than the blue paper-based paths.

5.1 Mobile Model in Enterprise Setting Work

There are myriad ways of configuring mobile work in an enterprise. We focus here on mobile professional work that has high payoffs in many enterprises. The mobile work model, as developed in Barnes (2004), consists of three axes – **Value, Mobility** and **Process** – and is particularly useful in developing

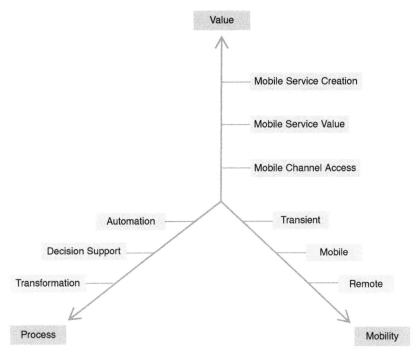

Figure 8 Mobile work model

opportunities of smartphone-based mobile work processes in an enterprise, as shown in Figure 8.

Value: This axis refers to creation of value to the enterprise or, to be precise, value proposition in the marketplace. It denotes the changes caused by mobility in its business offerings of products and services with respect to its customers and other stakeholders. This axis is divided into three levels:

- Mobile Channel Access is the lowest level where mobile medium is used primarily as a channel for information for mobile employees without any changes to the business services and products.
- Mobile Service Value is the intermediate level where the mobile solution adds significant value to the market offerings by the creation of distributed mobile work.
- Mobile Service Creation is the highest level where the business creates new services and products, as in the examples of Uber, Airbnb, Instagram, WhatsApp and the like.

Process: This axis describes changes in business processes as the effect of wireless work on configuration and makeup.

- Automation is the first level and denotes efficiency gained in the existing business processes by mobile work.
- Decision Support is the second level. At this level, mobile work provides increased effectiveness of knowledge provided to the professional worker at right time and place.
- Transformation is the highest level where a fundamental change takes place in business services and products, as in the cases of Uber, Airbnb and the like.

Mobility: This axel denotes the locational independence due to mobile work.

- Transient is the first level where employees move from one location to another where their work is performed, and they are tied to their locations.
- Mobile is the second level where employees have high degrees of independence in their locations, but they eventually return to their designated work locations.
- Remote is the highest level of mobility where workers are completely removed from their enterprise location and are empowered by access to enterprise data as required.

This model provides a phased introduction of mobile work into existing business and enterprises. It is useful as a framework to develop distributed mobile work formulation and for its analysis.

Enterprise mobility consists not only of mobile technologies but also of business context and access to business information to perform business processes independently from workers' locations. This requires accelerated business processes and high flexibility of workflows, thereby improving response time and reducing operational costs. Its aspects are geographical location independence, diversity of users and a host of supporting technologies required to enable it.

6 Mobile Moment Formulation and Fulfillment

High velocity business operations are made by creation of mobile moments of a business task and performing them on a handheld mobile device. We define a mobile moment as an event in time and space when someone takes out a mobile device to get what he or she wants immediately in context. This definition must be extended in view of current use of smartphones in business. Mobile moments occur whenever a person interacts with his smartphone for any task or event where an application provides menus and processes. Mobile moment interaction (also called engagement) with a stakeholder is important to accomplish in a given business task.

We define mobile moment interaction as a mobile business practice consisting of programmed sets of actions, processes, people and technologies to accomplish a business task at high electronic speed in real-time. Businesses must create and develop mobile moments for stakeholders like customers and workers and engage them with proper menus, messages, prompts and alerts; essentially, handholding stakeholders to accomplish desired business goals.

Mobile business moments are analogous to traditional business moments, like conventional face-to-face and paper-based business processes. Examples of such moments are 1. initiating purchase or work request, 2. obtaining status of a business process or a transaction or 3. requesting data and information and the like to complete a business task. However, mobile moments greatly differ from physical moments, since mobile moments exist in the digital world. Formulation and creation of mobility moments, and their fulfillment to meet business requirements, is the most important step in achieving a successful mobile business operation. It offers immense efficiencies, high-speed operations and new business opportunities.

6.1 Mobile Moment Creation and Engagement

Mobile moment creation and fulfillment comprises the following four steps as depicted in Figure 9. All the four steps must be considered together in formulating mobile moments for a specific business task.

The first step consists of charting mobile moments on a timescale of a task to be performed. This step is generally performed by a creative professional and or

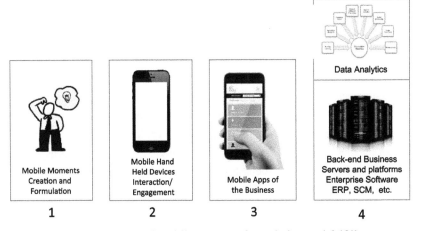

Figure 9 Four steps of mobile moment formulation and fulfillment

Ease of Mobile Moment Engagement	Leverage Phone Native APIs	Profuse Use of Corporate, Public, and Social Networking Data and Resources
Swipe Touch Voice Pen Keyboard GPS Sense Face Recognition 3D Gestures	Barcodes RFID GPS/Geo Fence Temperature Pressure Voice Calendar Camera/ Video Other Sensors	Timely Menus Messages Alerts and Alarms Data Mining Predictive Analytics Streaming Data Analytics Cross Promotion

Figure 10 Best practices of high velocity business app development

a business executive. Examples of such time lined mobile moments will be given later.

The second step consists of choosing some or all available mobile devices and how they will display mobile moments and interact with the end user. There are myriad handheld wireless devices, but only a few of them are pervasive and they offer ample choices of business applications. Current dominant devices are based on Apple iOS, Google Android and Microsoft Windows operating systems.

The third step is to create a mobile app that runs on chosen mobile devices and the fourth step is back-end analysis. The created mobile app must easily interact with the end user and must prompt the user with menus, alerts and messages to perform a specified business task. The mobile app must make use of mobile hardware resources as shown in Figure 10, with all business-accessible internally and externally stored and on-line resources.

The attributes for the best mobile app development are summarized in Figure 10, which provides guidelines to a would-be developer like ease of use, ability to gather and use information from diverse corporate business resources, social and public network data in real-time and often to capture high speed streaming data followed by intelligent analytics. Step 4 of Figure 9 represents this aspect in a concise manner. Specific focus to winning mobile moment interactions for a business includes the following:

- Serve the user wherever he is and whatever the time is with all your available business resources and DP capabilities.

- Anticipate the needs of the user with reference to the context and provide step-by-step guidance through menus, prompts, messages and alerts.
- Whatever the user action is, you should respond promptly by helping the user.

Mobile moment interaction with a customer should involve utilizing all available channels inside and outside an app. Push notifications play important role in higher user retention and satisfaction and they must be used to guide the user.

6.2 High Velocity Business Operations by Charting Mobile Moments

In this section, we illustrate how mobile moment charting provides high velocity business operations. In the current smartphone era, mobile moments are pervasive and universal for billions of people for various needs like finding a restaurant, getting a taxi, aiding air travel, mobile banking and payments, healthcare, company work, sports and in many other aspects of peoples' lives. But intelligent and smart handholding of a customer during the entire business service with engaging mobile moments is performed by only few industry front-runners. These are the high velocity business apps. Thus, opportunities to create proper smart mobile moments in many business tasks and perform them efficiently and at high speed are numerous. We provide a few examples to stimulate readers to further pursue them in their businesses or to start new businesses based on them (like new restaurant services, work tasks, Uber, Airbnb, Amazon and Google services).

In Figure 11, we show mobile moments in a generic restaurant scenario. It is a simplified example and it can be tailored to any restaurant by introducing more mobile moments for promotion, handholding and avoiding annoying factors to prospective customers. This Figure shows the timeline of a far-away customer locating the restaurant with driving directions and avoiding annoying busy parking spaces to timely arrival at the restaurant where the waiter creates memorable dining experiences.

Still another example is depicted in Figure 12 where the comprehensive needs of a business traveler are anticipated and addressed through the timeline of prior trip planning to any travel changes to check-in at the specified gate and disembarking at the destination with luggage pickup.

Creative formulation of mobile moments and their fulfillment will have to be carried out for a specific business and its goals and objectives in order to attain high velocity business operations. The primary idea is to help business stake-holders by handholding them and aiding them to perform their tasks with greater efficiency and speed. The implementation of world-class mobility in a business

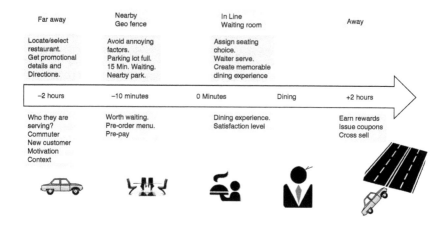

Figure 11 Mobile moment chart of a restaurant example

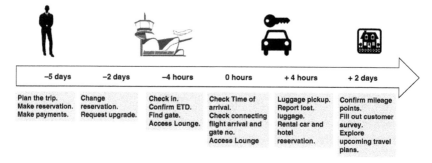

Figure 12 Mobile moments of a business traveler

requires mobility platforms or, in general, business platforms tuned to the business.

A well-conceived and suitably configured platform plays a vital role in high velocity business operations and is the primary enabler to achieving successful and competitive high velocity enterprise with mobile unwired operations. It is the cornerstone of high velocity business and its operations, therefore, we will deal with the platform in the next sections of this Element.

7 Platform Configuration and Concepts

Mobile platforms are basic enablers of high velocity business operations and necessary for successful and competitive business. Superior product alone is not enough to succeed in the current marketplace, as illustrated by the examples of Nokia and BlackBerry, which both failed in the marketplace, despite their superior products. Competitive iPhone and Android phones succeeded due to their platforms. Successful products must have well developed platforms for their market success. Therefore, high velocity business operations must be made on suitably configured mobile platforms. A high velocity business enterprise based on current well-developed smartphone platforms is a logical choice and therefore we treat in sufficient depth.

The word platform has been in use since 1574 or even earlier as per the Oxford English Dictionary, with essentially same meaning literally and metaphorically. It is a heavily used word in common usage as well as in many professional fields like technology, economics, business, sociology, and politics. It has disparate meanings and it has also many dimensions and perspectives which can define it. We focus here on technology, business and economic aspects of "Platform", as they are more pertinent to enterprise mobility. We define it as a structural framework or foundation on which a primary product or service stands in order to furthering the product and or the service developments with third-party innovations and collaborations. It provides a means to reuse many of its parts to develop the product and services intended for it. Furthermore, it provides a structural foundation to develop complementary products and services from third parties and as well as from the platform owners with heavy reuse of its components, thus minimizing efforts for further product developments. In addition to reuse of parts, it provides a competitive weapon to include or exclude some third-party products or services for competitive advantage as we will see it in later sections of this section.

A modern mobile device platform is an evolving system composed of interdependent modules that can be innovated upon with increasing interdependency of products and services as well as with increasing capability to innovate by many different actors. It is essential to maintain the platform integrity during its evolution and at all stages by a single driver/owner to ensure the product/service compatibilities.

Furthermore, platform provides an elevated stage for a product (or service) to be visible in a crowded marketplace along with its add-on complementary products for its enhanced utility. Well-developed platforms incorporate network effects to capture rapid market share and in some instances the winner takes the entire market as in the cases of Wintel platform which was formulated by Microsoft and Intel in early 1980s for PCs and Google Search platform in 1990s.

Platform concept in technical products is not new and it was known well over two centuries as in Railroad platforms (Broad Gauge, Meter Gauge and the like), Henry Ford's Model T car, Lego blocks, Credit Cards and the like.

In today's hypercompetitive world, even excellent products cannot stand alone for any length of time. They need platforms to support and nourish them in the marketplace, otherwise they will perish. Platform strategies are vital for any product or service to thrive. Nokia-Symbian, Research-In-Motion /BlackBerry and Palm Treo have had outstanding smartphone products with many first mover advantages, but all their products stood on crumbling platforms of poor design and development. Newcomers like Apple, Amazon and Google have built their products on superior platforms and hence were able to quickly out-compete these established incumbents. Scores of successful companies like Facebook, LinkedIn, eHarmony, Google, eBay and many others all have their products stand on superior platforms that they have carefully tuned and developed to suit to their products for excelling in the marketplace.

The smartphone is eminently suited to perform high velocity business operations, so we will discuss its platform in detail. It is a complex device that has its own extensive ecosystem encompassing several industries and services as illustrated in Figure 13. As obvious from this figure, the smartphone depends on multiple industry platforms to provide high velocity business operations – from basic materials to components and subsystems to system software and integration to wireless networks and applications.

The smartphone handset has many platforms – one as the main and others as supporting or sub platforms, including some nested platforms (i.e. platform in a platform). In Figure 14, we show the primary platforms of the smartphone handset classified as seven layers.

The platforms in the vertical stack shown in Figure 14 are basic to smartphone handsets and form the basis for performing high velocity business operations. They comprise hardware platform, operating system, external sensors and associated controllers (currently treated as subplatforms), network platform, application development platform, content delivery platform and

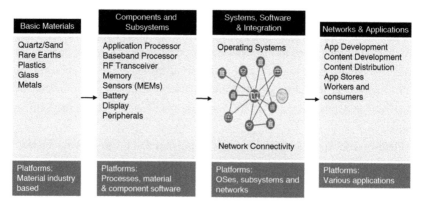

Figure 13 Versatile smartphone ecosystem for high velocity business

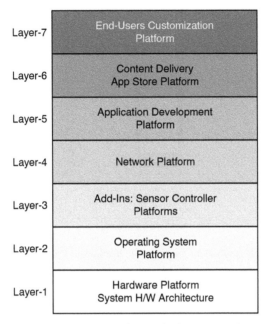

Layer-7	End-Users Customization Platform
Layer-6	Content Delivery App Store Platform
Layer-5	Application Development Platform
Layer-4	Network Platform
Layer-3	Add-Ins: Sensor Controller Platforms
Layer-2	Operating System Platform
Layer-1	Hardware Platform System H/W Architecture

Figure 14 Simplified smartphone platform seven-layer stack

end user customization platform as shown in the top layer of the Figure. High velocity business operations are developed and implemented on top of this seventh layer.

In addition, there are other application support platforms as shown in Figure 15, which include the important context engine platform which is essential in all high velocity business operations. Sensors and controller platform enable remote-work performance. Platforms of virtual reality, location and value exchange provide other useful business operations.

While the primary platform stack as shown in Figure 14 provides significant benefits to the handset maker (like customer lock-in and barriers to customer switch-in to other platforms), application support platforms offer revolutionary functionality for increased user experience. It is important to note that these application support platforms enable the business to formulate a "multisided platform" to bring together multiple interdependent groups of customers. It provides a business model where such platforms offer significant value to one group of customers if other groups of customers are prevalent. Google search is an example where it dynamically generates multisided platforms of search results of sites and searches. We will discuss more details of primary platforms and support platforms later, after discussing the fundamentals.

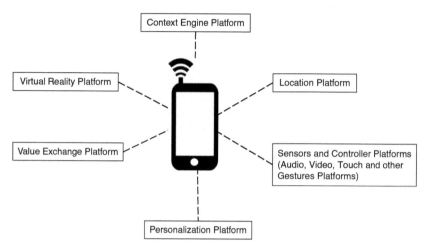

Figure 15 Examples of smartphone application support platforms

7.1 Platform Models

The primary role of platform services and products in mediating the actions of disaggregated firm ecosystems is now well established in the literature. There are diverse types of platforms that exist in a corporation, embedded across its products and services and in the form of multisided markets. Platform architectures modularize complex systems in which some components remain stable for extended period of times (like the platform itself) while other complementary components are made to vary in platform to accommodate new features and functions.

A few years ago, the platform was considered as a base framework for product development with standard modules and components it could be built upon (Suarez and Cusumano, 2008; Gawer, 2009). Currently, the platform is considered not only as a technology but also the outcome of a set of business relationships between actors in an ecosystem. Figure 16, as per Eisenmann et al. (2007), shows the current model of a simple two-sided platform that includes complimentary network effects. This structure is basic to understanding many aspects of platforms including those of multisided platforms which are prevalent in the smartphone ecosystem. This Figure depicts platform sponsor and platform provider stacks bidirectionally connected to demand-side users on the left and complementor supply side at the right of the figure. It shows cross-side network effects between users and complementor suppliers. These networks are developed to provide positive feedback between users and complementors.

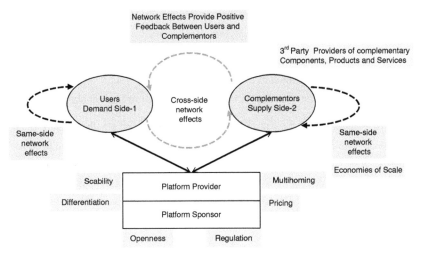

Figure 16 Current two-sided platform model

Current smartphones and other high-tech products and services are characterized as possessing high levels of interdependence between actors as well as high levels of innovation contributions by these actors. Even dominant players like Google, Samsung and Apple are dependent on innovation from platform actors for their prosperity in the marketplace. For example, for continued development, many Google and Apple smartphone applications and innovations are made by these external actors. Here the interdependence of the actors includes transactional supply-chain flow of products and services and as well as strategic interchange of integration of innovation among primary companies and their complementors to advance the platform.

In modern smartphones and wireless devices, platform is important and should be developed by considering individual business strategies and technology developments. Network effects play a vital role in a successful platform. Sometimes indirect network effects and technology paths are more important than direct network effects. We discuss the network effects as outlined in the Figure 16 in detail next.

7.2 Network Effects

Network effects were first realized in the early telephone industry in 1908 by Bell Systems' chief Theodore Vail and its researcher (Lytkins, 1917). Later, between 1985 and 1995, these effects were further advanced by Katz et al. (1985). Ralph Metcalfe (1980), the Ethernet pioneer, popularized the network effect in the early 1990s. Network effects act like a flywheel: the more you spin it, the more momentum you generate with faster and faster spins. In the smartphone ecosystem, network effects offer the following benefits:

- Exponential growth and value-creation opportunities;
- barriers to new entrants and competitors; and
- market opportunities for the winner to take the entire market share.

Network effects are different from the economies of scale that result from business size rather than inter-working. Economies of scale are on the production side and network effects are on the demand side of economics. Network effects have positive feedback and each additional user adds additional value to every user. There are also negative network effects, such as traffic congestion, and network congestion due to limited bandwidth and large numbers of users.

There are basically four types of network effects as follows (Arun, 2013):

1. Direct network effects as exhibited in two-sided platforms. An increase in subscription or usage causes a direct increase in value to other users, as in telephone systems, Skype, Facebook and the like.
2. Indirect network effects, which are common in software (Economides and Katsamakas, 2006). In this case, each user's adoption payoff, and incentive to adopt, increases as the number of complementary products or services increases. For example, a software application like Microsoft Word with its increased use causes corresponding increases in other applications like PowerPoint and Excel that belonging to a particular Windows operating system. Hence Windows OS is dominant over Linux. This effect is also known as a cross-side network effect, since advantages in one area cross across other areas.
3. Multisided network effects: This effect creates value by bringing two or more different types of economic agents together and facilitates interactions between them that make all agents profitable. It is often called the two-sided network effect, when there are only two economic agents. This effect is often found in application development platforms.
4. Local network effects: This effect is prevalent in social networks where subscribers benefit from local relationships of other subscribers. Instant messaging is an example of this effect. Here each user benefits from the local influence of a small subset of other users (Arun, 2007).

8 High Velocity Business Platform Development Factors

In today's hypercompetitive marketplace, it is essential to build high velocity business as well as its operations on sound platform factors. Multiple platforms and subplatforms are commonly involved in building a successful high velocity business. They are essentially mobile platforms with smartphone platform attributes.

It is important to focus on platform development, governance and maintenance matters, since mobile platforms like Google Android and Apple iOS played major roles in capturing billions of customers and millions of third-party developers who were instrumental in developing thousands of applications to their chosen platforms, which in turn provided viral market growth very quickly. Companies like Palm HP, Nokia and BlackBerry have mainly focused on developing and marketing superior products but suffered poor market performance and their platforms finally crumbled. The modern digital platform concept and its importance were realized only in the post–PC era after the first

Table 5 Conventional corporations versus mobile digital platform-based companies

Item	Pre–PC era conventional company	Post–PC era digital platform-based company
1. Competition	Static and slow competition, within the industry. Competitive takeovers are slow and generally within the business area.	Dynamic, open and fast competition. Due to network effects, competitors from unexpected areas can quickly overtake.
2. Business scope and analysis	Intra-industry business scope and analysis is only considered within the industry.	Inter-industry and ecosystem-level scope and analysis is required across many industries.
3. integration level	Tightly integrated within the company. Vertical integration of components and products within the company.	Dis-integrated with modular and complementary components and products from external companies.
4. Expense consideration	Transaction and agency costs.	Company-level capabilities.
5. Business model	Single invention innovation model within the company.	Multi invention and innovation model from several complementary and competitive companies.

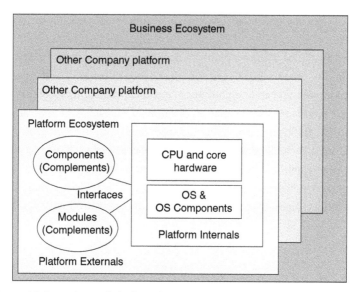

Figure 17 Overview of platform internals and externals applicable to high velocity business mobile device

IBM PC introduction in 1981. In the pre–PC era, corporations were operating in conventional classic business models where vertical integration of products and proprietary closed internal platforms comprising proprietary OSs and major modules and interfaces were common norms. Examples of such companies include Digital Equipment Corporation (DEC), Sperry Rand, IBM, Burroughs, Atari, Apple and many others. In IOt we show the differences of pre-PC conventional and modern post-PC mobile digital platform companies' operations.

Platforms are not products. They are intellectual-property creations developed by their owners and maintained by them to further their primary products. They consist of reusable components to enable quick economical development of new products and features. Their conception, architecture, development, governance and maintenance depend on individual companies' objectives (dependent on internals of the company), business ecosystem (which largely depends on externals to the company) and sound business practices.

In order to clarify platform development and governance aspects, we show platform internals, externals and ecosystem and how they must be structured, developed and deployed in Figure 17.

The basic architecture of any platform is essentially to design an inner core of the platform shown as platform internals where the system is partitioned into stable modular components; and a complementary set of platform ecosystem (also known as platform externals) with a high variety of variability to suit several individuals and entities with the capability to adapt to changing technologies and needs. However, platform interfaces are exceptions and they should be designed to be stable for extended periods.

Many platform pundits emphasize the reuse and sharing of core components of the platform; but it is only a tiny part of platform benefits. We believe that platform architecture that adds new features and functions to the product to cope up with changing technologies and markets offers significant benefits of the platform. Well-designed platform architecture enables not only the addition of new features, but also the ability to remove unwanted existing features to offer derivative products for market niches.

Well-built platform architecture satisfies the needs of a core group of customers and enables them to easily modify the platform to create derivative products through addition, subtraction or substitution of features and functions with appropriate platform interfaces, technologies and investments. It also provides competitive tools to triumph over other competing platforms through exclusion and or inclusion of third parties through formidable switching costs and deliberate blocking of competing platforms, and through network effects to gain external developers through attractive interfaces and APIs.

A platform is designed to maintain its core components with a set of design rules for stable constraints while fixing its interfaces between external components and its internals. As per Baldwin (2007), fixing interfaces between components creates specified thin crossing points in the network relationships between the elements of the system. Interface specifications provide dependencies between components and constrain them to the company objectives. Hence, interfaces establish boundaries of modules and components of the system whose "elements are powerfully connected among themselves and relatively weakly connected to elements in others" and thus define weak linkage points in a network of relationships for better coordination of transaction costs across the module boundary. Therefore, the platform provides a means to disaggregate corporate's product manufacture and allows external companies to participate in production with external innovations and skills. It is important to note that if these interfaces are not well-administered, the company can lose control to external companies. For example, the PC platform conceived by IBM in 1981 lost its platform control to component suppliers Microsoft and Intel with enormous loss of revenues over several years.

In developing a platform, it is important to consider platform evolutionary trajectory to sense whether it can adapt to unanticipated changes in external environments. In both man-made and biological platforms, evolution occurs via the mechanism of variation and selective retention of advantageous forms.

Darwin's seminal theory (Darwin, 1859) referred at length to biological system (which is essentially a platform) to establish variation as an empirical fact. In multicellular organisms, a wide variety of outward forms are accomplished through conservation of core metabolic processes at the cellular level. These core processes are naturally designed to conserve and minimize interdependence of processes while enabling complementary processes to support variation and facilitate adaptation. A similar scheme in man-made platforms is essential for superior evolutionary trajectory where the architecture partitions a system into stable core components and variable peripheral components. With reuse of core components, such partition will reduce the cost of variety and innovation at product and system levels. The entire system does not have to be reinvented or rebuilt from scratch to design a new product, accommodate a variety of needs or respond to external environment. In this manner, the platform as a whole is evolvable, and it can adapt at low cost without losing its uniqueness or continuity of design.

Platform adaptation to environmental changes is an important aspect for product survival, and how the platform architecture is designed to satisfy this requirement is important. Simple natural systems like bacteria vary their core processes, but there is a limit to complexity if every subsystem is changeable. In a complex system like a smartphone, where the system comprises many interacting parts, well-conceived platform architecture offers many benefits to cope up with evolving technology and a changing marketplace. It is important for the platform developer to know which components should remain stable and which should vary. The developer must be able to create stable and versatile interfaces that can accommodate future linkages unanticipated at the design stage.

8.1 Platform Management and Development Framework

In this Section, we will first outline the best practices in developing an outstanding platform as outlined by Gawer and Cusmano (2012). Later, we will detailed the guidelines of how to develop it. The steps involved in developing such a platform are as follows:

First Step: Develop business objectives and goals of how a product, technology or service will become an important ingredient of a bigger business ecosystem.

1. Determine (or design) an entity that has platform potential that performs an essential function and simple for other parties to interface to.
2. Find out potential external parties that could become complementors to the platform in different markets and applications.

Second Step: It is necessary to design the proper layout of the platform for a sound foundation with appropriate architecture and interfaces.

1. Embrace a hierarchical modular technical layout with simple and standard interfaces to facilitate third-party complementor innovations.
2. Share proprietary information rights on APIs and interfaces to platform modules with third parties to reduce their costs to take part as complementors to the platform.
3. Provide proper incentives to third-party complementors to participate in furthering the platform.

Third Step: Form an alliance around the platform with a shared vision for complementors to cocreate and innovate superior platform parts.

1. Clearly state a set of mutually rewarding business models for different actors to enhance the platform ecosystem with innovative and improved complements.
2. Publicize the merits and advantages of the platform layout.
3. Share risks and rewards with the complementors.
4. Foster strong alliances between the participants by the use proper forums.

Fourth Step: Layout platform evolutionary trajectory for both the short term and long term to outdo and outperform the competition and the marketplace.

1. Continue strong commitment and innovation of the platform core while maintaining its integrity to attract and continue third-party innovations and complements.
2. Lock in the participants and customers by making switching costs to other platforms expensive and difficult.

In developing the required platform, the owner must consider not only reusability of modules and components, but also platform evolution for short-term and long-term business needs. In order to accomplish platform goals, the platform developer must first plan the architectural foundations to properly delineate internals and externals and how third-party participants take part in codevelopment of complements and/or components for mutually rewarding business outcomes. The initial step is to define the platform internals and externals by way of aggregating their elemental components into modules to perform well-defined functions. Modules connect to other modules and other parts of the platform with well-defined interfaces. This step not only minimizes component complexity but also promotes modular interchangeability and standard interfaces. Most internal platform modules and components are generally protected

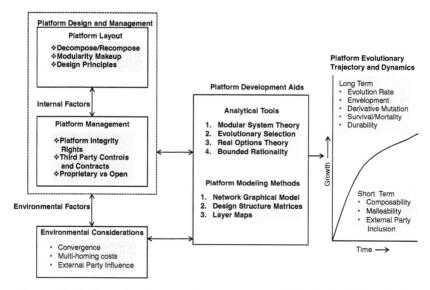

Figure 18 Platform development framework for mobile device high velocity business

as proprietary to ensure the platform owner's competitive advantage, while platform external modules are easily changeable and made open to third-party complements and innovations. These modules are connected to the platform with specified interfaces and APIs, which are provided to third-party participants under defined agreements, to facilitate their contributions to the platform.

We provide here important guidelines that are largely based on the work of Tiwana et al. (2010) and Baldwin (2008). In Figure 18, we show the platform development framework for proper management, deployment and maintenance, which provides broad guidelines for proper conception, development, maintenance, analysis and management of a platform.

In Figure 18, the platform design and management comprise platform layout and management, interfaced with internal factors. The details of these blocks are shown in the inner blocks. Environmental factors linking design and management of the platform comprise convergence, multi-homing costs and external party influence.

Platform development aids consist of analytical tools: modular system theory, evolutionary selection, real options theory and bounded rationality. Platform modeling methods involve network graphical model, design structure matrices and layer maps. They are discussed in detail in the following Sections.

8.2 Platform Layout

Platform layout is the first important step in conceptualizing a platform and describing its internal and external makeup. This step defines the platform architecture and its foundation. Furthermore, it partitions the platform into two parts – internals and externals – as shown in Figure 18. Internal components are made to be stable, less variable and highly reusable, whereas external components are made to be more variable and less reusable to meet the demands of new technologies and customers' and third-party participants' requirements. The internal and external components of the platform connect to one another with design rules binding them with the defined APIs and standard interfaces as depicted in the Figure. It is important to properly conceptualize and partition the platform according to the business requirements, since the steps taken here are often irreversible and the platform owner has to live with that layout for a long time.

The underlying principles of high velocity business platform layout and its architectural development are best understood from the epochal paper reference, Simon (1962). Although Simon's book deals with wide fields like physical, biological and social systems, it offers essential methods and processes for analyzing and developing current and emerging digital platforms as required for high velocity business ecosystem. We deal here with Simon's theoretical foundations and contributions and how they are applicable to today's platform layout in enough detail. It is important to note that (according to our in-depth investigation and interviews with Apple, Google, Microsoft, Amazon, Twitter, Facebook and scores of other companies' digital platforms developers and researchers during 2007–2012) current business and other digital platforms are developed by ad hoc trial-and-error methods rather than on sound principles and processes as described by Simon.

A complex system like a high velocity business platform is composed of a large number of parts that interact in a specified manner. In such a system, the whole is more than the sum of the parts; essentially, given the properties of the parts and their interaction processes, it is difficult to infer the whole.

Any complex system, whether natural or physical (like modern business), comprises many elemental parts that repeat with a certain frequency and form a hierarchy; the system has subsystems and so on, which in turn are also hierarchical. An example of a physical system are elementary particles making an atom, atoms making a compound, compounds making a complex substance and so on. A symbolic system example consists of alphabets, alphabets into words, words combined into sentences, sentences combined into paragraphs and so on. A biological example is cells making a tissue, tissues making an organ, and organs making body parts, or, in the other direction, a cell is defined by nucleus, cell membrane, microsomes etc. A digital complex system is a smartphone ecosystem platform that is composed of elemental electronic and mechanical components, in hierarchical levels of basic modules, and aggregated basic modules into parts and subfunctional modules, and subfunctional modules grouped into functional modules and so on to build the smartphone and its platform. This aspect tells us how to breakdown a complex system into its elemental entities and how to recombine and organize them into hierarchical modules. Simon proves that hierarchic systems are stable and long-lived, whereas nonhierarchical systems are unstable and short-lived.

An important property of the complex system is its layout and how that is related to the system's evolutionary trajectory and how the system adapts to the changing future to survive and thrive. Simon concludes that a well-organized hierarchical system evolves quickly with little effort, whereas a nonhierarchical system evolves very slowly and with great difficulty. A hierarchic system is composed of interrelated subsystems, each of which in turn is also hierarchic, until we reach a lower level elementary or atomic subsystem. The basic property of the hierarchic system is its depth, indicating the levels of hierarchy, and breadth, indicating its horizontal span. Some hierarchical systems are flat with one or two levels and some others are deep with multiple levels. The span of hierarchy varies from system to system.

Well-thought-out hierarchic organization of components, submodules and modules is very important in business platforms as illustrated by marketplace facts: poorly organized hierarchical systems, as in Palm, BlackBerry, and Nokia-Symbian, were unable to compete with better-organized hierarchical systems like Android and iOS. Of course, Android and iOS could be even better organized if they utilized the rigorous processes developed by Simon rather than by the trial-and-error methods the platforms currently employ.

Simon provides a convincing discussion and proof of the importance of hierarchy in evolution by providing examples in many biological, physical and other systems, but the parable of the two imaginary watchmakers is very convincing and its extension to the mobile platform scenario is obvious. Hora and Tempus were two watchmakers of the industrial era who were equally talented and produced watches with about 1,000 parts each. Hora prospered but Tempus failed, although both made excellent watches. Tempus assembled all the 1,000 pieces one by one and if he had to put it down, it fell back into its 1,000 basic parts and he had to begin again. Hora, on the other hand, adapted a hierarchical structure in building watches, designing his manufacturing process such that ten elements could be made into one subassembly, and ten of these subassemblies later constituted a larger subassembly, and ten of these larger subassemblies made the whole watch. Production interruptions are common in any manufacturing process, but if Hora was interrupted while working on a partly assembled watch, he could put down the subassembly in order to address the interruption and he lost only negligible work, thus assembling his watches in a fraction of the man-hours that Tempus required.

By assuming the probability of interruption as 1 in 1,000 (p=.001) Simon quantitatively computes the relative difficulties of Hora and Tempus as 1 to 4,000 with some approximations in their watch assemblies. Hence the Hora's hierarchical organization of the assembly process of provides a 4,000 to 1 advantage over Tempus' nonhierarchical assembly process. Since a typical smartphone platform comprises multimillion components, proper hierarchical organization of submodules and modules is essential for a successful business operation. Imperfections in hierarchical organizations of smartphone makeup will thus result in enormous differences in efficiencies of operations.

8.3 Decompose/Recompose

Platform decomposition comprises breaking down its form and functions into its atomic components, which is important in understanding and analyzing the platform and improving it by way of optimally recomposing its atomic parts into hierarchic modules. New conceptual platforms, existing platforms and other world-class competitive platforms can be analyzed by their decomposition and later they can be reconstituted to improve them to suit to the changing business and for competitive advantage. Simon's analytical process as outlined in his 1962 paper provides basic steps for decomposition and for recomposition into hierarchical modules. A platform can be hierarchically decomposed into smaller subcategories until further decomposition reaches the elemental/atomic level and does not provide any meaningful information. The number of subsystems of a platform defines the span and the number of sub-sublevels determines the depth of the hierarchy.

Decomposition allows the developer to determine which modules should be internal to the platform and which others should be outside the platform echo system. It provides a method to dis-integrate the platform so that external participants can further advance the platform. Furthermore, decomposition minimizes interdependence so platform modules can be independently developed without interference from other modules.

It is interesting to note that some varieties of systems can be approximated as nearly decomposable systems. It is a limiting case of a nonhierarchic system, where the span of hierarchy is one and all submodules are independent with no interaction among them, but the modules can be interdependent and independent. In such a system, all modules can be put outside the platform to enable third-party developments of the modules. Such a system becomes a open system with public participation. The Linux-based platform is one such example.

8.4 Modularity

Modularity is defined as "the degree to which a system's components can be separated and combined" (Schlling, 2000). It refers to not only the extent of component coupling but also to the design rules of combining the components. Baldwin and Clark (2000) define modularity as "a structural means of achieving functional integration in complex systems." They provide three features of modularity:

1. Modules are distinct parts of a large system;
2. Modules are independent of one another; and
3. Modules function as an integrated seamless whole.

A complex high velocity business platform comprises of several parts that interact and are independent to some degree. These parts are commonly arranged in a hierarchical organization composed of interrelated subsystems which in turn may have their own subsystems and so on. Simon's 1962 paper defines a nearly decomposable system where interactions among systems are weak. The essence of this structural decomposition is to localize environmental disturbances within a specific subsystem and not to propagate them across the entire system. Modularity creates a high degree of independence between component designs by standardizing component interface specifications.

Modularity is important to a complex system, like a smartphone platform, where its components can be separated and recombined. It refers to exchangeable parts in assembling the platform. With modular design, the platform components can connect, interact or exchange signals in some manner by adhering to interface specifications. In a tightly integrated system where modularity is zero, each component is designed to work specifically with other components in a tightly coupled manner, whereas in a modular design the components are loosely coupled. Modularity offers three important advantages:

1. Make complex system more manageable by a divide-and-conquer approach;
2. Allow parallel work by independent parties with minimal (or no) coordination; and
3. Accommodate future uncertainties and innovations. In a modular design, new module designs can be substituted for older designs at lower efforts.

There are six modular operators that can be applied to a modular system as per Baldwin et al. (2003):

1. **Split**: Divide an independent system or module into modules and/or submodules;
2. **Substitute**: Replace one module with another;
3. **Eliminate**: Exclude the module from the system;
4. **Supplement**: Add a new module to the system;
5. **Inversion**: Collect common elements across several modules and organize them as a new level in hierarchy, creating new design rules and structural modules; and
6. **Port**: Make a module compatible with two or more systems, creating a shell around a module such that it works in other systems.

These operators operate in pairs. Appropriate use of these modular operators in a platform ecosystem provides significant economic and technical advantages as demonstrated by Baldwin and Clark (2003). For example, splitting and substituting a complex system into x modules provide 2x alternative options, thereby providing more choices for better selection. Both products and processes are treated as modules and thus the six operators are extended to process modules. The modular operators are employed to create new modules that create new products, processes and services.

A pictorial view of operation of the six operators provides a better understanding of how they can be used in a modular platform as per Figure 19, which is essentially based on Baldwin and Cross's (2003) example, with minor simplification for clarity and some variations in terminology. In Figure 19a, we show a simple two-level generic hierarchic system with six modules (A, B, C, D, E, F). In Figure 19b, we apply the six modular operators as depicted to arrive at the final three-level hierarchic system. Module A is split into three, A1, A2 and A3, as shown in Figure 9.8b. Three different substitutes were developed for Module B. Module C was eliminated as marked my X. A new module G was developed to supplement the system. Common elements of Modules D and E were inverted as shown in the Figure. Subsystem design rules and architectural modules were developed to enable inversion operation. Module F was ported. First it was split, later its inner modules were grouped within a shell. Later translator modules were developed. The resulting system is a three-level system with two modular subsystems performing the functions of the old system modules A, D and E.

Such modular operations can improve platform quality by way of increasing choices and by more favorable economic operations.

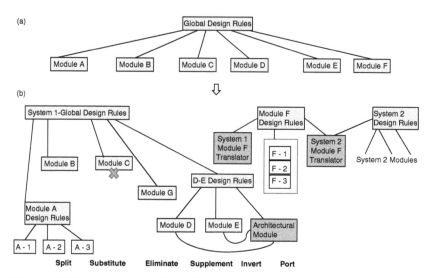

Figure 19 Simple example of modular operators on a 2-level hierarchic system yielding a 3-level hierarchic system

In a perfectly modular subsystem, changes made in one module will not affect other modules and parts of the system. On the other hand, in a low modular system, changes made in one module will cause ripple effects in other parts of the ecosystem. Platform modularity can range from low to high modularity. Modularity is developed by increasing decoupling between modules and by way of platform–module interface standardization. Decoupling hides a behavior in which internal changes in a module or a part do not affect other parts of the platform ecosystem. Increasing modularity decreases coordination and transaction costs across the module boundary as elaborated in Baldwin (2000).

9 High Velocity Business Platform Design Principles

It is important that business platforms, tasks and operations follow proper design rules and principles to further increase their velocities. We provide such design principles here.

Design principles are dictated by the platform owner to include design rules and policies that platform developers and third parties must comply with in order to ensure platform interworking and integrity. Two important attributes of these design principles are 1. how stable these principles are relative to the platform life cycle; and 2. how versatile they are to accommodate changes and future innovations. Stable design principles ensure that platform module developers do not have to learn new principles and they can be assured that their developed modules and parts continue to comply with the platform ecosystem. Too much stability may hinder coping with future innovations and new developments. Therefore, the platform designer must consider this dichotomy of too stable versus adaptable to change. The designer must balance stability and inclusion of flexibility and versatility by anticipating forthcoming innovations and new technologies.

In order to design and develop modular parts of the platform, a technique called design structure matrix (DSM) mapping and its applications are useful (Eppinger and Browning, 2012). DSM is essentially a two-dimensional matrix representation of the structural or functional interrelationships of objects, tasks, components, processers or teams. DSM was successfully used by Sun Microsystems in developing Java platform modules for well over two decades and in PC-computer systems circa 1993. It describes a variety of applications and examples relevant to smartphone platforms and other various situations like components, activities, interactions, interfaces, tasks, people and the like. We will focus here on smartphone platform modules and components as some typical examples.

DSM is a useful networking tool to show platform modules and elements by highlighting the architecture. DSM is represented as an N x N matrix mapping the interactions among the set of N elements. In a simple binary case, only 1 and 0 is used to represent whether interaction exists between the elements or not. In advanced DSM models, a range of values can be assigned, but we will deal here with the simple binary N squared matrix (Figure 20).

Figure 20 illustrates components along the Y-axis and four modules with components as shown. The X-axis represents design parameters or component interactions. DSM modules can also represent processes, people, organizations and others other than assembly of components as shown in the figure. Here we show poorly configured modules with substantial interactions among components of other modules; inter-module component interactions are also predominant.

Optimum platform design requires the least number of inter-module component interactions, so that third-party developers can easily participate in platform development. Figure 21 shows an idealized platform configuration where intra-module component interactions are at a minimum; and there are more intra-module interactions.

Figure 21's platform configuration can be obtained by appropriate rearranging of components and specifications of interfaces to the modules by complying with the design principles. A DSM-based tool called a nonconformity matrix (NCM), as developed in Travers et al. (2013), is useful. Application of DSM on NCM tools enables identification of clusters of non-

Component Interactions/ Design Parameters

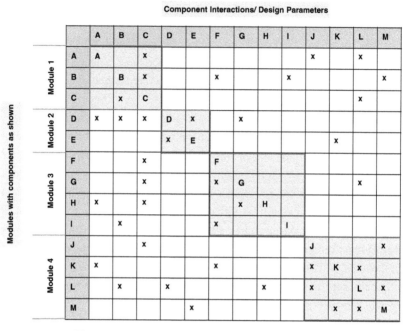

Modules with components as shown			A	B	C	D	E	F	G	H	I	J	K	L	M
	Module 1	A	A		x							x		x	
		B		B	x			x		x					x
		C		x	C									x	
	Module 2	D	x	x	x	D	x		x						
		E			x		E						x		
	Module 3	F			x			F							
		G			x			x	G					x	
		H	x		x			x		H					
		I		x				x			I				
	Module 4	J			x							J			x
		K	x					x				x	K	x	
		L		x		x			x			x		L	x
		M					x					x	x	x	M

Figure 20 Initial DSM platform module analysis

Component Interactions/ Design Parameters

Modules with components as shown			A	B	C	D	E	F	G	H	I	J	K	L	M
	Module 1	A	A	x	x										
		B	x	B	x										
		C	x	x	C										
	Module 2	D	x			D	x								
		E			x		E								
	Module 3	F						F	x	x	x				
		G						x	G	x	x				
		H	x					x	x	H	x				
		I						x	x	x	I				
	Module 4	J										J	x	x	x
		K	x									x	K	x	x
		L										x	x	L	x
		M	x									x	x	x	M

Figure 21 Desired DSM platform module analysis

conformities and provides leads to improve platform quality. NCM comprises ten steps:

1. Identify and define the problem to be analyzed;
2. Identify all non-conformities in the platform ecosystem modules;
3. Collect and analyze all relations and interactions between non-conformities with clear description about each dependency;
4. Transport all data to DSM, parsed by platform deployment processes and evaluation of final DSM;
5. Employ mathematical operations like clustering and sequencing algorithms to the DSM and evaluate the final DSM;
6. Perform design experiments based on the previous selection of what are the critical quality characteristics as per response variable under analysis;
7. Refine the development and deployment processes as per item 6 results;
8. Reevaluate the relations of non-conformities and eliminate them as appropriate;
9. Update and evaluate DSM; and
10. Refine the model over successive iterations.

This 10-step process was successfully applied in a manufacturing process, but it is equally applicable to platform development and deployment processes. It is important to note that a typical smartphone platform contains hundreds of components and tens of modules and the resulting DSM is several times larger than the DSM shown in the Figure 21 example.

10 Platform Management

Platform management involves making decisions about all aspects of the platform as to how to design and evolve it, how to use and apply it and, importantly, how to share ownership rights of its parts with third-party stakeholders. This involves what proportion of rights and exclusive ownership of the platform should belong to the owner, and how much should be given to external third parties for their participation and furthering the platform. Too little will discourage third-party participation and too much will result in eventually loss of the owner's control of the platform and perhaps loss of the platform itself, as happened when IBM lost control of the IBM PC platform case to Microsoft, Intel and other third parties like PC makers Dell, HP, Acer, Asus and the like. On the other hand, maintaining excessive ownership rights and providing only few rights to the third parties, as done by Nokia-Symbian, Palm Treo and BlackBerry, is also undesirable since external parties may not have enough incentives to further the platforms, which has led to poor performance of these platform products in the marketplace. Thus, provisioning the correct balance of rights is an important aspect of platform management. There are three distinct aspects of platform management:

1. dividing decision rights,
2. control, and
3. proprietary versus shared.

These aspects provide a sound basis for managing sharing responsibilities and rules of the platform, aligning incentives to third-party contributions in proportion to their efforts and actions, and sharing revenues of the platform outcomes.

10.1 Dividing Decision Rights

Dividing decision rights involves how decision authority is shared between the platform owner and other stakeholders like module developers, application providers and component makers. Decision rights consist of who has authority and responsibility for making specific decisions in terms of the platform parts. There are three basic components to decision rights:

1. Who should decide the functions and features of the module? Should it be a shared responsibility between the owner and an external developer?
2. Who should decide how the module is configured, designed and implemented with proper user interfaces; and
3. Who should control platform internal interfaces, since the interfaces are more lasting and stable than the platform itself? Control over these interfaces means control over the platform and its evolution.

Thus, dividing decision rights involves how the platform owner and module developers share these three components. The details of these decision rights are ratification (i.e., approval authority of modules functions); authority to specify and implement performance measurement criteria with reference to the platform; authority to use the extent of system resources; and implementation decisions about approved modules or executing ratified functions.

Dividing decision rights creates problems due to fragmentation of autonomy between platform owner and module developer, but their outputs need to be integrated into the platform for mutual advantage. Thus, the correct balance must be maintained between the owner and developer in dividing these rights. Excessive division of rights involves more coordination and more use of external innovations and minimal division involves more owner control with less reliance on external innovations.

10.2 Control

Control is seeing that everything specified or agreed upon is carried out appropriately. It involves ensuring current performance meets pre-determined objectives. According to Koontz (1980), control is the measurement and correction of performance in order to make sure that enterprise objectives and the plans devised to attain them are accomplished. Control is a continuous process.

Proper control methods and processes for the platform ecosystem is important, since poor control can result in loss of benefits and development, as in the case of Nokia-Symbian, Palm Treo and IBM PC platform. The platform owner must consider control mechanisms for platform inputs, outputs and interfaces.

Control processes and mechanisms must be carefully set up so as not to discourage external third party participation and at the same time to maintain control over the platform. The relationship between the platform owner and the module developer is not the classical principal–agent relationship, since the platform owner does not contract the developer to participate in platform module development.

Control mechanisms can be unidirectional or bidirectional, but quite often they are in the form of coordination mechanisms between the owner and developer. Platform inputs, outputs and interfaces can be better controlled by coordination and bidirectional control processes for the mutual benefit of the platform owner and the external stakeholders. An important aspect of platform management is to include optimal control mechanisms whose attributes are directionality, variety and degree of use of various control mechanisms.

Proprietary versus Shared

Platforms can be proprietary, like Apple iOS, where a single owner controls it; or, as in the case of Google's Android, be shared by many parties. This attribute is different from open versus closed architectures: for example, Linux is open source and Apple iOS is not only closed but also proprietary. This attribute has a significant role in platform evolution where either a single party or multiple parties develop to further advance.

Internal Factors

Internal interfaces and architecture are important to connect to third-party modules. They determine the environmental evolution of the platform. A wide choice of attachable and substitutable modules that are easily interfaced to a given platform product provides much wider network effects (positive or negative) for the successful placement of the platform in the marketplace. In order to accommodate unknown future developments, the platform internals must be flexible for successful coevolution of platform management.

Environmental Considerations

Platform environmental factors external to it – like other competing platforms, third-party developers and customer base – always change with time. They play a major role in platform positioning in the marketplace, as do technological developments and changes.

Convergence

Technological convergence in data, video and voice can seriously impact the platform and a platform owner can embrace such convergence positively for penetrating adjacent markets for greater market share. There can also be a negative impact on platform evolution dynamics from competition by relevant new overlapping platforms. However, more opportunities abound to make use of such increased developer and user bases with multiproduct bundles and "envelopment" potentials (Eisenmann et al., 2011). Platform envelopment means one platform-field owner entering another platform-field and its market by combining its own functionality with the targets to form a multiplatform bundle, essentially, swallowing another adjacent platform owner. Envelopment strategy enables capture of a share by foreclosing an incumbent's access to users and thus harnessing the network effects that previously helped the incumbent. Three categories of envelopment are currently known as envelopment of unrelated platforms, envelopment of weak substitutes and envelopment of complements.

Multi-Homing

Developers and users consider homing costs of platforms important, since these costs comprise the aggregation costs of adoption and operation and opportunity costs like learning platform tools, APIs and other usage procedures. Multihoming, which involves switching from one platform to another, must be kept simple and attractive since many developers and users prefer multi-homing to take advantage of different platforms strengths. It must include compatible interfaces, APIs and standards.

Multi-homing provides opportunities to make use of other platforms' developers and users, where cross-switching costs of platforms are made negligible and homing is made attractive with features and functions. When competing platforms lower their switching costs by offering attractive pricing and tools to their platforms, module developers begin to migrate to them as per "tipping," described by Katz and Shapiro (1994).

Party Influence

External parties include component suppliers, developers and other stake-holders such as service providers. There are inherent tensions between external parties and the platform owner due to divergent interests and financial goals, and careful balancing is necessary. Platform evolutionary dynamics largely depends on managing such diverging interests.

11 Platform Development Aids

Platform development aids are tools that provide deeper perspectives about the platform. They are analytical tools that enable the platform owner to better configure, design and develop the platform. They are 1. modular system theory; 2. evolutionary selection; 3. real-options theory and 4. bounded rationality.

11.1 Modular System

We have previously discussed modularity in detail, so here we highlight its salient attributes as a tool that will assist us to formulate better platforms. The basic premise of modular system theory is that a complex system, like a mobile platform, comprises smaller subsystems which interact in a predefined manner with standard and stable interfaces to the platform. Such a modularized platform is easier to manage, produce and change than a monolithic platform.

Modularization of a platform provides cross module and core module independence. This allows subsystems to independently evolve without any coordination efforts or having to know the internal details of the subsystems. Modularization provides the following four benefits to the platform owner.

1. Significant reduction in coordination costs between module developers and platform owners by offering embedded coordination mechanisms (Sanchez and Mahoney, 1996).
2. Reduction of efforts in managing and developing modules by reducing cross-module and module-to-module integration costs.
3. Increased module developer autonomy by substituting formal process control with that of the module developer's procedures and methods.
4. Decreased module developer task boundaries, thus providing the developer deeper specialization of the field.

11.2 Evolutionary Selection

The mobile platform is a complex ecosystem with hierarchical organization of subsystems, sub-subsystems and components and so on. It is analogous to many biological systems that are also hierarchically organized as cells, tissues, muscles and organs and the like. Therefore, its evolution is somewhat like a complex biological system evolution.

A more complex hierarchical modular system evolves faster with better environmental fit than a monolithic or less hierarchical system as per Herbert Simon. A complex system, with its diversity of modules and components, has many choices for evolutionary paths and, as such, it evolves faster than other systems that do not possess these characteristics. In the smartphone case, the more diverse Google Android platform is evolving faster with better environmental fit than platforms like BlackBerry, Palm Treo and the like. Slow evolution is detrimental to human-made platforms and biological systems due to their lag in environmental fit. High diversity in a nearly decomposable system provides ample evolutionary recombination schemes, leading to faster evolution and better environmental fit. A system is nearly decomposable if it consists of parts that interact weakly with one another and the parts in turn are made of smaller parts with similar properties. For a rigorous mathematical analysis of such systems, see Simon (2002).

11.3 Real Options Theory

The mobile platform environment is characterized by high levels of competition, rapid change, great uncertainty and the need for flexibility and, as such, it is important for a platform owner to employ real-option theory and its associated tools and processes. Real-option theory has been well developed over the past five decades (with contributions from many Nobel laureates) to account for both uncertainty and the platform owner's ability to react to new information on technologies and markets (see Guthrie [2009] and Brosch [2008]). Real option means to the right to do some act without the obligation to perform it. It offers future flexibility with its value correspondingly increasing with uncertainty and a longer time interval over which it can be exercised.

Real option theory is very effective in high velocity operation development and smartphone platform development due to its explicit recognition that future decisions designed to maximize value will depend on new information, such as forthcoming technologies and marketplace conditions, acquired over an exploratory period. Real option is based on the future value of the core underlying asset (in the smartphone case, this is its platform) and the future value of the investment. Several strategic and operational real options can be embedded in a platform at the upfront option expense and each must be exercised at the opportune time to reap the maximum benefits of the option.

Real options benefits can only be realized by deliberately embedding them into the platform development process and exercising them at a suitable future time. The six previously mentioned modular operations of splitting, substitution, augmentation, exclusion, inversion and porting identified by Baldwin et al. (2003), embed different types of option-like flexibility, each of which can have a greater value when external conditions pose greater uncertainty about the platform environment.

Real options can be used in three distinct modes (or approaches) as follows:

1. As a conceptual thinking tool where real options are used mainly as a language to frame and communicate decision problems in a qualitative manner;
2. As an analytical tool to pricing option models to determine valuation of projects with defined option characteristics; and
3. As a management tool to identify and make use of strategic options.

For detailed discussions of using real options in these three modes and case studies, see Triantis and Borison (2005).

11.4 Bounded Rationality

Bounded rationality is applicable to platform design, development and implementation, since these things are complicated and involve large amounts of data and information. As there are numerous researches, literature and books on bounded rationality, we provide brief outline of it and refer the readers to Gigerenzer and Selton (2002) and Simon (2008).

Decision makers work under three unavoidable limitations: 1. Often only incomplete and unreliable information and data is available; 2. Humans have limited capacity to process and evaluate information and data; and 3. Only limited time is available to make decisions. Hence, decision-makers are bound to attempt rational choices in complex situations with insufficient research and data. In design and development of smartphone platforms, these three limitations invariably occur due to the complexity of the platform containing several thousands of subsystems modules and components. The huge number of platform ecosystem parts exponentially increases the interdependencies and interferences among them.

Decision analysis is fundamental to platform development and, as such, bounded rationality in decision-making plays an important role. Rational decision processes involve making decisions with all information and with perfect models. However, in practice, it is extremely difficult to have all necessary

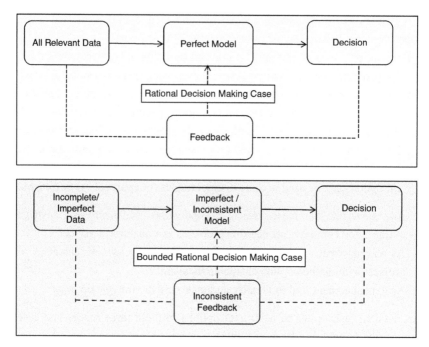

Figure 22 Rational and bounded rational decision-making models

perfect information and perfect knowledge of the models. In Figure 22, we illustrate a rational decision-making case and a bounded rational decision-making case. The upper block of the Figure shows rational decision-making case with all relevant data and with a perfect model. The lower block shows bounded rational decision-making case with incomplete and imperfect data with imperfect model.

Bounded rationality as shown in Figure 22 consists of the cognitive limits of individual developers with reference to their capabilities to process and interpret large quantities of relevant data. As a smartphone platform ecosystem grows in complexity, the number of interdependencies with the platform grows exponentially and it is necessary to employ bounded rationality by way of acquiring enough data with good-enough solutions. Previously provided design rules, such as the design structure matrix, and best practices with models, will narrow the scope of information, while bounded rationality-based decisions provide high accuracy.

12 Makeup and Constitution Analysis of Mobile Platforms

Mobile platform evolutionary dynamics depends not only on external but also internal agents. Path dependence theories and researches deal mainly with

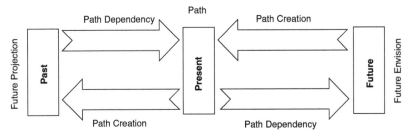

Figure 23 Duality of path creation and path dependency

external observers. Path creation deals with the actions of internal agents such as platform developers and entrepreneurs. A combination of path development and path creation is important to fully understand smartphone platform dynamics. Path constitution comprises path dependency and path creation as defined by Jorg Sydow (2012).

In mobile device development, iPhone platform creation (made by Apple entrepreneurs and developers led by Steve Jobs) played a major role. It is important to note that this path creation was dependent on the paths previously developed and created by touch-screen pioneers during the past half century, as well as previous mobile phone technologies. Without these technologies, the iPhone platform would not have been created.

Path dependence and path creation are intimately intertwined – two sides of the same coin – interrelated to past, present and future as shown in Figure 23.

Referring to Figure 23, path dependency is charted from past to present, small changes matter in terms of chaos theory and history matters. Past path creation is carried to the present for future vision and path creation. This figure uncovers three important aspects: 1. Path dependency will not only propel the present but also influences the future by way of path creation; 2. Path dependency and path creation determine the present and give birth to each other; and 3. Path dependency and path creation interact with one another and give rise to unique business opportunities.

Path dependence focuses on past events and realizes the importance of self-reinforcing processes that are activated by one or more small events and chart the evolutionary path. Paths are non-ergodic with the possibility of different outcomes at the start but at the mature end-stage, the possibilities narrow down to equilibrium with none resulting in a locked-in state. Self-reinforcing processes follow the law of increasing returns thus resulting in a locked-in state.

Path creation, as introduced by Garud et al. (2010), focuses on the importance of the efforts of multiple competent individual and organizational actors and, in particular, of coordination of their activities with one another. Path creation studies mainly consisted of case studies, and therefore Sydow (2010) formulated path constitution analysis (PCA), providing a sound formal basis.

Path constitution is a combination of path dependence and path creation and it is defined as a course of events interrelated on different levels of analysis, such as a single organization or an organizational or technological field, in which one of the available technological, institutional or organizational options gains momentum in time-space. Path constitution analysis by has six components:

1. Level of interrelatedness defines a focal level of analysis required to conceptualize relative to surrounding levels of analysis comprising micro and macro elements.
2. Triggering events defines certain incidents that potentially cause the current and or future trajectory of a path.
3. Non-ergodic processes defines the course of simultaneous and/or sequential events resulting in an outcome that was indeterminate from the onset.
4. Self-reinforcing processes defines a course of interlocking simultaneous and/or sequential events that are progressively aligned to each other, thereby aiding the overall trajectory path leading to a momentum.
5. Lock-in defines an outcome where the trajectory path converges to equilibrium with a single solution that may not necessarily be efficient.
6. Multiple actors are constellations of individual or collective agents who have a stake in the outcome.

PCA provides a sound methodology to analyze mobile device platforms and to further develop them to position them in the marketplace for highly competitive advantage.

13 Mobile Platform Analysis

Mobile platforms are evolving in two different ways determined by their underlying foundations: 1. based on a handset operating system and its associated stack of platforms where each operating system wants to control its own stack; and 2. based on the convergence of wireless telephony with internet services, personal computing services and a myriad of mobile devices like wireless wearables, wireless sensors and sensor networks, where open standards control the stack. Both foundations depend on a same vertical stack of platforms, where each layer is intimately interdependent on the other layers of the stack.

The first foundation preserves the proprietary nature of a handset operating system and its associated platform architecture. The second foundation is based on open platforms and technologies, where proprietary smartphone operating systems are made irrelevant due to open internet services and

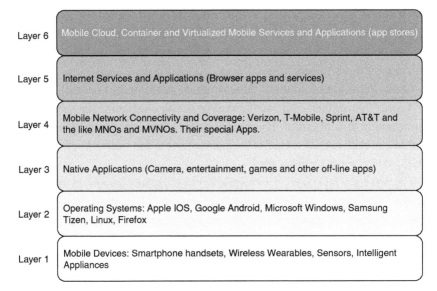

Figure 24 Mobile device platform stack

applications. These two foundational approaches have two very different business objectives and goals. The first foundation approach relies on the proprietary OS foundations of the handset like Google's Android, Apple's iOS and Microsoft's Windows. The second foundation approach emphasizes open services where mobile internet standards, mobile application virtualization, mobile cloud computing and services provide technologies and solutions to accommodate any mobile device operating system. It is important to note that, in either approach, virtualization schemes can be applied to broaden the smartphone applications where proprietary handset operating systems become less relevant. In Figure 24, we show the mobile device platform stack that accommodates these two fundamental platform evolutions. They consist of six layers as shown. The first layer is the basic mobile device; the second is the operating system; the third is native applications; the fourth is mobile network connectivity and coverage; the fifth is internet services; and the sixth is mobile cloud and virtual mobile services. It is important to make high velocity business operations over the fifth and sixth layer to take advantage of lower layers.

In order to strive and succeed in the marketplace, smartphone platforms must broaden across horizontal stack elements as well as vertical stack elements. They must become mobile device platforms rather than the current smartphone platform stacks in order to support not only smartphones but also a variety of mobile devices as seen in Figure 24. Apart from wearables like smart watch, smart shoes, smart eyeglasses, a wide range of smart appliances like smart refrigerators, washing machines, home thermostats and controllers, wearable sensors and sensor networks that require platform support are also rapidly entering the marketplace.

Unlike PCs, PDAs and tablets, the smartphone platform stack has more layers and many independent and interdependent actors interacting and intimately coordinating their offerings. These independent actors independently innovate and advance the state-of-the-art of the mobile devices and smartphones. We will briefly describe the platform stack.

The first stack layer comprises mobile devices and their associated hardware as shown in Figure 24. The second layer consists of smartphone operating systems, which are important platform builders. Handset manufacturers make the operating system as an essential element to lock in customers and build proprietary features to not only differentiate their products, but also to gain competitive advantage. They do this by increasing the switching cost and dominating the market by reaching equilibrium of the path evolution as discussed in previous sections of path dependence and path creation. They also lock in customers from layer six by using mobile cloud services for their App stores, from which they can deliver their streaming-media of audio and video and other apps. Layer three provides native services offered through the operating system software.

Layer four offers mobile network connection services and associated network applications offered by MNOs and MVNOs – corporations like Verizon, T-Mobile, AT&T, Walmart and the American Automobile Association. These companies also lock in customers to their own networks and prevent them from using other MNO–MVNO networks. Layer five provides internet connectivity and services offered through mobile browsers. This layer depends on internet standards and it is open to all customers as per internet rules and principles. Layer six network services are offered by mobile clouds which are built on top of the Internet.

Google and Microsoft use not only their operating systems but also their search engines' strengths to differentiate their products and services to lock in customers. Mapping and GPS network services are also leveraged by these companies.

13.1 Mobile Application Categories

Mobile applications can be classified into three categories based on their behavior and how they make use of the underlying resources of the handset and Internet and Web resources.

1. Native applications reside entirely in the handset and efficiently make use of all underlying smartphone resources like camera, microphone and other various sensors. These applications do not depend on the Internet and hence they can run without any wireless connections. Camera, listening to stored music, audio recording and many games are some examples. These applications are specific to a particular platform and they do not work on other platforms. They can only be supplied by the handset maker or its App store.

2. Web applications are written in internet browser HTML language and other internet resources. As such, they work on any platform. However, they require internet connectivity with an appropriate browser. The advantage of these applications is that they can be distributed through the Internet without the platform owner needing an App store.

3. Hybrid applications make use of native handset resources as well as internet resources and they are essentially a combination of these two categories.

The decision to select a category of application depends on several factors. Some critical factors include:

- Does the mobile application require the use of special handset device features like its camera, flash, accelerometer, microphone or other sensors?
- Does the mobile application need to be internet connected to make use of some internet resources?
- How important is speed and performance?
- What programming languages the developer already know?
- Does the application have to be targeted to several platforms?

13.2 Operating Systems of Mobile Platforms

In current state-of-the-art smartphone operating systems play an important role in mobile platforms. Currently, three mobile device operating systems dominate the marketplace, each with its own strengths and weaknesses and each able to equally satisfy customer needs as required. They are Microsoft Windows, Google Android and Apple iOS platforms. With reference to consuming needs and ease of use, Apple iOS dominates and with reference to productivity purposes and professional needs Microsoft Windows OS offers superior benefits. Android OS offers both productivity and ease of use for consumer applications. Figure 25 shows these three operating systems as they dominate the mobile device platforms.

It is important to note that with some minimal effort, any one of these OS platform can perform both productivity and consuming applications to satisfy

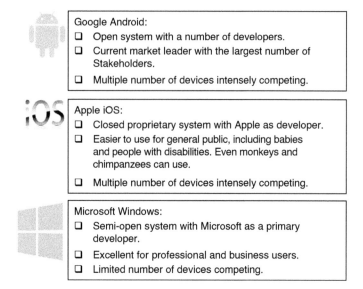

Figure 25 The three dominant mobile device platforms

the needs of consumers, professionals and productivity personnel. Each platform is evolving to widen its field of applications as well as specialize in their own niche applications.

Currently, as it stands, Microsoft Mobile OS is eminently suited to enterprise and business applications with its well-developed connectivity and compatibilities to many professional and business programs like AutoCAD, CRM and ERP software, and professional productivity software such as Microsoft Office with numerous scripts and templates for any business use. With many PC server software products and with thin client interfaces suited to mobile devices, the Microsoft platform is an eminent choice for business and professional apps.

Apple's iOS platform is the best choice for ease of use for general consumers and even for children and the disabled because of the many intuitive user interfaces. It has been demonstrated that even chimpanzees and other monkeys and animals are also able to use some of its applications.

The Android platform is designed for a wide variety of devices and applications and stands in the middle for consumer and business productivity applications. It is a widely adopted platform with many stakeholders independently innovating and advancing the platform.

Any one of the three smartphone OS operating platforms, or a combination of them, are excellent to serve high velocity business operations. These platforms can further be integrated with internal business platforms to offer many real-time high velocity business services.

14 Examples of High Velocity Business Operations

In the previous sections, we covered the fundamental principles and methods of configuring and designing efficient high velocity business operations with mobile moments and their associated platforms of how to implement them with well-configured and well-designed processes. Here we provide representative examples of high velocity business operations in different fields with their benefits analysis.

Businesses perform and rely on real-time events and data collected by pertinent sensors that are stored along with past events and data. High velocity operations use this data with fast processing, retrieval and communication with relevant entities with minimal latencies. Latencies occur due to technical solutions that have delays in data capture, storage in databases, retrieval of relevant data from storages and actions taken. The higher the velocity of operations, the lesser will be latencies with higher values to the business in general. It is important to choose the right latencies and optimum velocity for each business operation as the case requires, since very low latencies and very high velocities of operations are expensive due to the cost of high-speed computer processing technologies, high velocity communications and faster databases. However, these high-speed computing and communication costs are coming down rapidly due to innovations in their architectures and chip technologies, making many high velocity operations more cost effective today than in the past. In Figure 26, we show value of high velocity operations versus latency of acting.

In Figure 26, we have shown latencies due to five broad categories: 1. event capture involving sensor reaction and responses; 2. data storage delays in writing data to a database; 3. relevant data retrieval involving read and write delays; 4. data transfer delays due to communication delays depending on the distances of relevant parties and devices; and 5. acting on information according to business requirements and rules. These five latencies add up and contribute to delayed actions. In many cases, data is not stored in one place and obtaining it from multiple sources causes more latencies. Similarly, computing in analyzing resources may be performed at several locations, such as cloud computing facilities and local servers, which causes more latencies.

In emergency situations, such as warfare scenarios and medical conditions, it is critical that latencies be kept very low. High velocity operations are often necessary to address them. Similarly, in autonomous navigation and robotic operations, these latencies should be minimized. In several business operations such delays can incur lowered costs and lost opportunities. We broadly classify

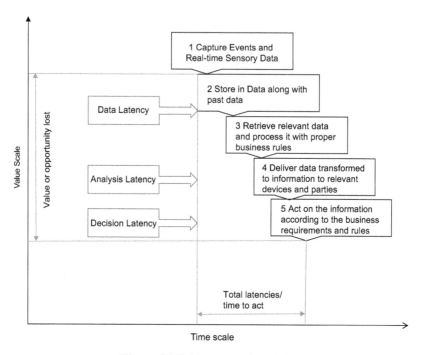

Figure 26 Value versus time delay

three cases where these five combined latencies cause difficulties for the business:

Critical: Not meeting a certain specified time will have catastrophic consequences;

Useless: The information is useless after the specified time; and

Decreased Value: Information decreases in value after the specified time, but is still of value.

14.1 Common Use Cases of High Velocity Business Operations

We briefly describe two common use cases of high velocity business applications and list others in Table 6.

Production Operations Improvement: In manufacturing operations, new processes are always introduced and executives determine output and input goals depending on customer demands and orders based on their past records. Previously, inputs and demands were estimated based on the historical data that generally provide rough figures.

Table 6 Importance of high velocity business operations triggered by IoT, 5G, AI and big data analytics

Broad category/ field	Typical applications	Remarks
Industrial IoT and smart factories	Remote factory work through smart sensors and actuators; robotic operations as in car manufacturing; remote process automation.	Factory automation, remote work in factories, speeding many business and factory operations.
Autonomous vehicles	Self-driving cars such as the Tesla and others forthcoming, remote vehicle communications; preventive maintenance; fleet management etc.	Must have real-time and faster-than-real-time predictive analytics.
Smart city	Real-time traffic control; water distribution; waste management; security and surroundings monitoring.	Must have real-time and faster-than-real-time business operations.
Connected health	Connected doctors and patients; instant emergency care; remote surgery; monitoring and medication e-care etc.	Must have real-time and faster-than-real-time business operations.
Smart farming	Smart irrigation; remote automated farming; cattle tracking; precision farming inch by inch and detecting water leakages and preventing them.	Labor saving with high efficiencies.
Emergency services	Early fire detection and prevention; flood indication and prevention; personnel emergencies	Preventive and real-time care.

Table 6 (cont.)

Broad category/ field	Typical applications	Remarks
Robots and drones	Real-time work and exploration in hard-to-reach and dangerous places.	Must have real-time and faster-than-real-time business operations.
Virtual reality and augmented reality	Exploring and taking proper actions on focused visual objects with greater sensory data. Examples are remote surgery; rescue in inaccessible and dangerous areas; and proactive policing.	Must have real-time and faster-than-real-time business operations.
Smart home and appliances	IoT is adopted in smart homes as smart lighting, home security and in several appliances. These connected devices interact and cooperate better with high velocity operations.	High velocity operations provide increased value.
Smart grid and power management	Efficient energy supply to homes and businesses; quick-charge stations for electric vehicles; power outage prevention.	High velocity control signals to make and manage electric energy packets like internet data packets.

With more timely and accurate estimation of demands in real-time, it is practical to determine operational inputs (rather than relying on estimates as in the past) to accurately produce just enough units to meet demand, which results in a continuous cycle of improvements in operations. This will stream-line inventories and supply-chain management for significant reduction of expenses.

Freight Management and Real-Time Order Tracking: In the past, order tracking started only when the items reached a certain point, resulting in uncertainty in the supply chain and challenges in determining the optimum allocation of work resources. With current technologies such as IoT and RFID tags, factory supervisors can now track items right from the factory floor to the customer premises in real-time with great precision. This coordinates the entire supply chain efficiently resulting in significant improvements to the business operations.

In addition to these two common cases, high velocity business operations have applications in many fields and in most such applications they are essential and in others they increase efficiencies and effectiveness. These high velocity operations are becoming pervasive due to adoption of emerging standards and technologies of Internet of Things (IoT), 5G, AI and big data analytics. For details of these technologies and applications, see Tripathy and Anuradha (2018), Nishith and Bhandari (2018) and Bahga and Madisetti (2016). High velocity business operations are important to make IoT applications practical and successful, as in self-driving cars, remote robotic operations, emergency health, remote expert surgeries and remote factory tasks. These operations are briefly listed in Table 6. The proliferation of these applications is changing the way we live, and work.

14.2 Makers and Drivers of High Velocity Operations

In this Section, we briefly describe makers and drivers of high velocity business operations resulting from emerging technologies and standards.

IoT technology and standards provide a new connectivity of things – everything to everything, connecting objects to objects and to people enabling many high velocity operations. The IoT ecosystem comprises net-works of sensors, actuators and smart objects, including factory objects in a manner to make them smart, intelligent and programmable. Therefore, there are ample opportunities for high velocity business operations in many fields, as shown in Table 6.

5G technology and standards provides high-bandwidth, low-latency wireless network connectivity for IoT objects. It provides several orders of magnitude higher bandwidth, which correspondingly improves velocity of business operations. It facilitates many new high velocity business operations and applications with its low-energy connectivity and the high velocity communications offered by its high bandwidth.

5G is more than a high-speed mobile network. It is a facilitator and enabler of applications in factory automation, robotics and AR/VR-based consumer and industrial applications. It is creating a new era of connecting people to things and machines at high-speed bandwidth with low latency and low energy levels to offer smart traffic and roads, autonomous vehicles, drones and planes and other applications as in Table 6.

AI and **data analytics** go together to create more novel and useful high velocity applications. One such example is real-time translations of multilingual conversations and dialogs as implemented by Google in their Android phones. In such translations, high velocity operations are essential.

5G and IoT create massive connectivity of devices, which in turn create massive data that is useful to facilitate industrial automation, robotics, AR/VR applications and remote work processes. Data analytics play an essential role to make use of the static massive data of databases together with real-time massive data for executable actions across several fields of industries. AI is becoming a general-purpose technology (GPT) in all fields of human activity and business and, as such, it is finding a vital role in these fields. The AI maturity application model is listed depending on the extent of applying AI in various applications.

Simple Context Sensitive Applications: This is the case in many prevailing applications as asset management and service reminders.

Predictive Applications: This is the case in prevailing applications like revenue forecasting and output forecasting.

Prescriptive Applications: This is the case in emerging applications like job scheduling and intelligent routing.

Cognitive Applications: This is the case in the emerging applications like in autonomous vehicle driving, and control and automation of tasks.

With increasing maturity of AI applications, the speed of business operations also increases and the importance of high velocity business operations. Many high velocity business operations are taking place due to AI and its deep learning as pioneered by Google, IBM and others. Deep-learning apps are in many cases more accurate and faster than humans in recognition of objects, persons and images. This is particularly helpful in, for example, IBM Watson Health applications for diagnostics. Many such novel high velocity business operations will continue to be developed.

The emerging world of our business and everyday dealings is increasingly based on high velocity operations. The new world is very different from the past and differences between customers, producers, suppliers, designers of products and service providers are blurred due to high velocities and disappearing distances and boundaries. The world, as well as businesses defined by space, time and mass, are thus very different and the new real-time and faster-than-real-time operations are providing us numerous benefits and vistas not known before.

References

Andriessen, Erik J. H., and Vartiainen, Matti, *Mobile Virtual Work: Concepts, Outcomes and Challenges*, 2010, Springer Verlag Publishing.

Bahga, Arshdeep, and Madisetti, Vijay, *Big Data Science & Analytics: A Hands-On Approach*, 2016, ISBN: 978–0996025539, Arshdeep Bahga and Vijay Madisetti.

Baldwin, Carliss Y., "The Architecture of Platforms: Unified View," Working Paper 09–34, 2008, Harvard Business School Reference.

Baldwin, Carliss Y., "Where Do Transactions Come From? Modularity, Transactions and the Boundaries of Firms," in *Industrial and Corporate Change*, pp. 1–41, December 2007, Industrial and Corporate Change Advance Access .

Baldwin, Carliss Y., *Design Rules: The Power of Modularity*, 2000, MIT Press.

Baldwin, Carliss Y., and Clark, Kim B. "The Value, Costs and Organizational consequences of Modularity," May 2003, Working Paper Draft, www .people.hbs.edu/cbaldwin/DR1/DR1Overview.pdf.

Barnes, Stuart J., "Wireless Support for Mobile Distributed Work: A Taxonomy and Examples," 2004, IEEE Proceedings of the 37th Hawaii International Conference.

Brosch, Rainer, *Portfolios of Real Options (Lecture Notes in Economics and Mathematical Systems)*, Apr 9, 2008, Springer Publisher.

Castells, Manuel, *The Rise of the Network Society*, pp. 327–468, 1996, Blackwell Publishers.

Damelio, Robert, *The Basics of Process Mapping*, 2011, CRC Press.

Darwin, Charles, *On the Origin of Species by Means of Natural Selection, or the Preservation of Favoured Races in the Struggle of Life*, November 1859, Appleton and Co., Publisher

Economides, Nicholas, and Katsamakas, Evangelos, "Two-Sided Competition of Proprietary vs Open Source Technology Platforms and Implications for the Software Industry," *Management Science*, Vol. 52, No. 7, pp. 1057–1071, July 2006.

Eisenmann, Thomas R., Parker, Geoffrey, and Van Alstyne, Marshall, "Platform Envelopment," *Strategic Management Journal*, Vol. 2, No. 12, pp. 1270–1285, April 2011. https://doi.org/10.1002/smj.935.

Eisenmann, Thomas R., Parker, Geoffrey, and Van Alstyne, Marshall, "Platform Networks-Core Concepts," Executive Survey, Paper 232, June 2007, MIT Center for Digital Business, http://digital.mit.edu.

Eppinger, Steven D., and Browning, Tyson R., *Design Structure Methods and Applications*, 2012, MIT Press.

Garud, Raghu, Kumaraswamy, Arun, and Karnoe, Peter, "Path Dependence or Creation," *Journal of Management Studies*, Vol. 47 No. 4, pp. 760–774, June 2010, Blackwell Publishing.

Gawer, Annabelle, *Platforms, Markets and Innovation*, 2009, Edward Elgar Publishing.

Gawer, Annabelle, and Cusmano, Michael, *Industry Platforms and Ecosystem Innovation*, 2012, DRUID, CBS, Copenhagen.

Gigerenzer, Gerd, and Selten, Reinhard, *Bounded Rationality: The Adaptive Toolbox*, 2002, MIT Press.

Guthrie, Graeme, *Real Options in Theory and Practice*, July 2009, Oxford University Press.

Hurkmans, Gert, and Van Elsen, Willem, 2012, "A Qualitative Review of Usability Studies in Higher Educational Programs in Digital Media in Belgium and Netherlands," Proceedings of ICERI 2012 Conference, November 2012, Madrid, Spain.

Kapoor, Amita, *Artificial Intelligence for IoT: Expert Machine Learning and Deep Learning Techniques for Developing Smarter IoT Systems*, 2019, Packt Publishing Ltd.

Katz, Michael L., and Shapiro, Carl, "Systems competition and Network Effects," *Journal of Economic Perspectives*, Vol. 8, No. 2, Spring 1994, American Economic Association.

Katz, Michael L., Shapiro, Carl, Farrell, Joseph, and Saloner, Garth, "The Implications of Network Effects for Competition Law," https://blog .ipleaders.in/implications-network-effects-competition-law/.

Koontz, Harold, "The Management Theory Revisited," *Academy of Management Review*, Vol. 5, pp. 175–187, April 1980.

Kristofferson, S., and Ljungberg, F., 2000, "Mobility: From Stationary to Mobile Work," in *Planet Internet*, pp. 41–64.

Lytkins, N., "Capacity Media-lobal Telecoms News, Events and Community," 1917, www.capacitymedia.com/articles/2758438.

Metcalfe, Ralph, "Compatible Communicating Devices," 1980, https://en .wikipedia.org/wiki/Metcalfe%27s_law.

Mol, Annemarie, and Law, John, "Regions, Networks and Fluids: Anaemia and Social Topology" *Social Studies of Science*, Vol. 24, pp. 641–671, 1994, Sage.

Nishith, Pathak, and Bhandari, Anurag, "*IoT, AI, and Blockchain for .NET,*" Aug 15, 2018, Apress Media LLC.

Sanchez, Ron, and Mahoney, Joseph T., "Modularity, Flexibility, and Knowledge Management in Production and Organization Design," *Strategic Management Journal*, Vol. 17, No. 52, pp. 63–76, 1996, Wiley.

Schlling, Melissa A, "Towards a general modular system theory and its application to interfirm product modularity," 2000, www.academia.edu /11758729_in_Multiple_Disciplines.

Sharp, Alec, and Mcdermott, Patrick, *Workflow Modeling: Tools for Process Improvement and Application Development*, 2008, Artech House.

Simon, Herbert A., *Economics, Bounded Rationality and Cognitive Revolution*, 2008, Edward Elgar Publications.

Simon, Herbert A., "Near Decomposability and the Speed of Evolution," *Industrial and Corporate Change*, Vol. 11, pp. 587–599, June 2002.

Simon, Herbert A., "The Architecture of Complexity," *Proceedings of the American Philosophical Society*, Vol. 106, No. 6, December 1962.

Somayaji, Nanjunda, Snehal, Meshram, Krishnamoorthy, Sudarshan, and Jayachandra, Y., *Smartphone Frontiers: Technologies, Applications and Markets*, 2014, McGraw-Hill Education.

Spear, Steven J., *The High Velocity Edge: How Market Leaders Leverage Operational Excellence to Beat the Competition*, May 2009, McGraw-Hill Publishers.

Steinberg, Randy A, *High Velocity ITSM*, 2016, Trafford Publishing.

Suarez, F. Fernando, and Cusumano, Michael A, *The Role of Services in Platform Markets*, 2008, The MIT Center for Digital Business, http://digital .mit.edu.

Sundararajan, Arun, "Network Effects," 2013, www.revolvy.com/page/Arun-Sundararajan.

Sundararajan, Arun, "Local Network Effects and Complex Network Structure," *The B.E. Journal of Theoretical Economics*, Vol. 7, 2007, New York University.

Sydow, Jorg, "Path Constitution Analysis: A Methodology for Understanding Path Dependence and Path Creation)," *German Academic Association for Business Research (VHB)*, Vol. 5, No. 2, Nov. 2012.

Tiwana, Amrit, et al., "Platform Evolution: Coevolution of Platform Architecture, Governance and Environmental Dynamics," *Information Systems Research*, Vol. 21, No. 4, pp.675–687, 2010.

Travers, S. M. O., Farooq, A., Araujo, A., and Novoa, H. "Application of Non-conformity Matrix", *FAIM*, Porto Portugal, 2013.

Triantis, Alex, and Borison, Adam, "Real Options: State of the Practice, *Journal of Applied Corporate Finance*, Vol. 14, Issue 2, 2005, Wiley Publisher.

Tripathy, B. K., and Anuradha, J., *"Internet of Things (IoT): Technologies, Applications, Challenges, and Solutions*, 2018, CRC Press; Taylor and Francis Group.

Vainio, Teija, et al., "Exploring the Transformation of Interaction in Mobile Work Contexts", *iJIM*, Vol. 2, April 2008, Elsevier.

Cambridge Elements ⹀

Business Strategy

J.-C. Spender
Rutgers Business School
J.-C. Spender is a visiting scholar at Rutgers Business School and a research Professor, Kozminski University. He has been active in the business strategy field since 1971 and is the author or coauthor of seven books and numerous papers. His principal academic interest is in knowledge-based theories of the private sector firm, and managing them.

About the series
Business strategy's reach is vast, and important too since wherever there is business activity there is strategizing. As a field, strategy has a long history from medieval and colonial times to today's developed and developing economies. This series offers a place for interesting and illuminating research including industry and corporate studies, strategizing in service industries, the arts, the public sector, and the new forms of Internet-based commerce. It also covers today's expanding gamut of analytic techniques.

Cambridge Elements ☰

Business Strategy

www.ingramcontent.com/pod-product-compliance
Ingram Content Group UK Ltd.
Pitfield, Milton Keynes, MK11 3LW, UK
UKHW020454010325
455719UK00016B/586